Quick to Knit

Knitting for Babies

Publications International, Ltd.

DESIGNERS: Lesley Edmondson (pages 36, 46); Chrissy Gardiner (page 74); Susan Leitzsch (page 67); Kathy Perry (pages 64, 82); Helen Ralph (page 88); Lucie Sinkler (pages 34, 49, 52, 57, 60, 85); Cathleen Stephen (page 70); Beth Walker-O'Brien (pages 40, 76, 92)

TECHNICAL EDITOR: Jean Lampe
ILLUSTRATOR: Joni Coniglio
PHOTOGRAPHY: Josh Dreyfus/ Josh Dreyfus Productions, Inc.
PHOTO STYLING: Lisa Baruch
ADDITIONAL PHOTOGRAPHY: © Deborah Van Kirk (page 4)
MODELS: Jade Benavides; Amber Elder; Elijah Farbrother; Maya Gougis; Kennedi Greer; Maxwell Jenkins; Gabriella Mazzara; Sahil Mittal; Analise Moran; Stella O'Connor; Michael Racanelli; Lily Rubin; Samantha Taylor

ISBN-13: 978-1-4127-1341-2
ISBN-10: 1-4127-1341-2

Manufactured in China.

8 7 6 5 4 3 2 1

Contents

Knit Wise!

So you've been wanting to learn to knit? Look no further than these simple step-by-step instructions with clear, easy-to-follow illustrations. *Knitting for Babies* is the perfect tool for any first project, and it gives you tons of fabulous options. Your only dilemma will be choosing which to make first! Read on—you'll be hooked in no time.

Casting On

The cast-on row is the foundation row of knitting. There are many ways to cast on stitches. One method may be easier for you to do, or it may work better for certain techniques, such as buttonholes. Try each of the following cast-on methods, and start with the one that most appeals to you. **Note:** The cast-on should be as elastic as the body of your knitting. If needed, the cast-on may be worked using a needle two or three sizes larger than your gauge needle. Knit the stitches onto the smaller needle as you knit the first row.

Making a Slipknot The first stitch on your needle for most cast-on methods is a slipknot.

Step 1: Hold the yarn in your left hand about 8″ (20cm) from the end. With your right hand, make a circle with the yarn *(fig. 1a)*. If it's helpful, hold the circle between your index finger and thumb to prevent it from slipping.

Making a Slipknot

Fig. 1a

Fig. 1b

Fig. 1c

Step 1: In your left hand, hold the needle with the slipknot. Hold the working yarn in your right hand. Insert the right needle through the slipknot from front to back and wrap the yarn around the right needle from back to front *(fig. 2a)*.

Step 2: With the working yarn behind the circle, insert the knitting needle through the circle from front to back and catch the working yarn, pulling it through the circle to form a loop *(fig. 1b)*.

Step 3: With the new loop on the needle in your right hand, gently pull both ends of the yarn (the tail and the working yarn attached to the ball) beneath the needle, then pull on the working yarn to tighten the new loop so that it fits snugly around the needle *(fig. 1c)*.

Cable Cast-on This cast-on is especially good when you need a firm edge. Work loosely, without pulling the stitches too tight.

Step 2: Pull up a loop with the working yarn, creating a new stitch on the right needle. Insert the left needle tip into the new stitch *(fig. 2b)* and slip it onto the left needle. There are now 2 stitches on the left needle. **Note:** To prevent the cast-on edge from becoming too tight, insert the right needle from front to back between the 2 stitches on the left needle before

Cable Cast-on

Fig. 2a

Fig. 2b

Fig. 2c

Fig. 2d

tightening the yarn. Gently pull the working yarn to tighten the stitch.

Step 3: With the right needle in position between the 2 stitches on the left needle, wrap the yarn around the right needle as shown *(fig. 2c)*, and pull through a new loop.

Step 4: Using the tip of the left needle, slip the new stitch from the right needle as before *(fig. 2d)*, and slip the right needle out of the stitch.

Repeat steps 3 and 4 to cast on additional stitches. End with step 4 to complete the last cast-on stitch.

Long-tail (or Slingshot) Cast-on The benefits of this cast-on method are that it's quick to do and makes an elastic edge. Both working yarn and tail are used. The tail length should be roughly three times the width of your desired cast-on, or about 1″ (2.5cm) per stitch for worsted weight yarn, plus several inches extra for the yarn tail allowance to weave in later. If you underestimate the length of yarn tail needed, pull out the work, add more yarn to the length, and begin again. Or,

begin the cast-on using two balls of the same yarn: One serves as the tail, and the other is the working yarn. Tie the ends together in an overhand knot, leaving about a 6″ (15cm) tail, make the slipknot as usual, and then begin the cast-on. When the cast-on is completed, cut one of the yarns, leaving about 6″ (15cm), and begin to work with the other. When the garment is finished, untie the overhand knot and weave in the loose ends.

Step 1: Place the slipknot onto the needle in your right hand, with the yarn tail in front (closest to you) and the working yarn (attached to the ball) behind the needle. Pull the working yarn taut over the left forefinger, and wrap the yarn tail around your thumb from front to back. Secure both the working yarn and the tail between the remaining three fingers of your left hand and palm. Place the forefinger of your right hand on top of the slipknot to hold it in place *(fig. 3a)*.

Step 2: Insert the needle under the yarn in front of your thumb, working from front

LONG-TAIL (OR SLINGSHOT) CAST-ON

Fig. 3a

Fig. 3b

Fig. 3c

SIMPLE CAST-ON (BACKWARD LOOP CAST-ON)

Fig. 4a

Fig. 4b

Fig. 4c

to back and pulling the yarn slightly upward *(fig. 3b)*. Insert the needle over the yarn on your forefinger, moving from top to bottom so the working yarn lies on top of the needle to form the new stitch.

Step 3: Pull the needle toward you through the loop on your thumb as you remove your thumb from the loop *(fig. 3c)*. At the same time, pull down on both pieces of yarn, tightening the stitch by pulling on the tail, keeping the stitch firm and even but loose enough to slide easily.

Repeat steps 1–3 to cast on additional stitches.

Simple Cast-on (Backward Loop Cast-on) This cast-on is probably the easiest to learn, but it doesn't have a neat edge like other cast-ons. Use it when working a few cast-on stitches or on buttonholes. This cast-on tends to grow longer and become less manageable as you work the first row of knitting because the cast-on stitches tighten, making it difficult to insert the needle.

Step 1: Place the slipknot on a needle with the yarn tail in back and the working

yarn in front. Hold this needle in your right hand.

Step 2: Wrap the working yarn over your left thumb from back to front. Secure the working yarn between the third finger of your left hand and palm to add tension and hold it in place *(fig. 4a)*.

Step 3: Insert the needle under the yarn looped around your thumb, working from bottom to top *(fig. 4b)*. Pull up on the needle a little as you slide the yarn off your thumb and onto the needle.

Step 4: Gently pull on the working yarn to tighten the new stitch on the needle *(fig. 4c)*.

Repeat steps 2–4 to cast on as many stitches as desired. End with step 4.

Knitted Cast-on This cast-on is easy to work and is very similar to the cable cast-on *(see page 5)*. The difference between the cable cast-on and the knitted cast-on occurs after the first stitch is made.

Step 1: Place the slipknot on a needle and hold the needle in your left hand, with the working yarn in your right hand. Insert the right needle through the slipknot from front to back.

The Knitty-Gritty

Knit Loops and Purl Loops

Before you venture any further, look at these six illustrations. They will help you understand many things about knitting, so study them well and plan to return to this page often. When a cast-on or stitch pattern specifies working into the front loop or back loop, simply match the instruction to the illustration to see exactly which part of the stitch is being described.

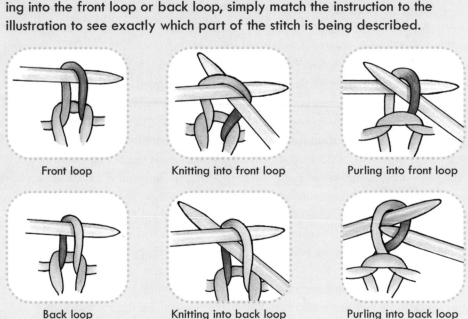

Front loop	Knitting into front loop	Purling into front loop
Back loop	Knitting into back loop	Purling into back loop

Step 2: Wrap the yarn around the right needle from back to front and pull up a loop, creating a new stitch on the right needle (*see fig. 2b, page 5*). Insert the left needle tip into the new stitch. Both needles remain in the new stitch.

Repeat step 2 for each new stitch until all cast-on stitches are made. Withdraw the right needle after the last stitch is made. Although both needles remain in the new loop at all times, the stitches collect on the left needle only.

Crochet Chain Cast-on The crochet chain cast-on and a standard bind-off look the same: a horizontal chain of stitches. Therefore, it's a good idea to

8

CROCHET CHAIN CAST-ON

Fig. 5a

Fig. 5b

consider this method when making scarves, afghans, baby blankets, and anything else where the cast-on and bind-off edges are visible in the finished item.

Step 1: Place the slipknot on a crochet hook and hold it in your right hand.

Step 2: Take the working yarn in your left hand, placing the knitting needle over the working yarn and under the crochet hook.

Step 3: Yarn over the crochet hook *(see page 17 for yarn over instructions)*, draw a loop over the knitting needle and through the slipknot *(fig. 5a)*, and take the working yarn under the needle (1 stitch on knitting needle, 1 loop on crochet hook).

Step 4: *With the working yarn under the knitting needle and the crochet hook over the needle, yarn over the crochet hook and draw the yarn through the loop on the crochet hook *(fig. 5b)*, and take the working yarn under the needle (1 new stitch on needle, 1 loop on crochet hook).

Repeat from * until the required number of cast-on stitches are on the needle, slipping the last stitch from the crochet hook onto the needle.

The Basic Stitches

Knitting has two basic stitches: the knit stitch and the purl stitch. After mastering these stitches, you'll be able to create many stitch patterns.

Knitting is enjoyed all over the world, but not everyone likes to knit in the same style. There is no right or wrong style of knitting. This book presents one of the more common knitting methods used in the United States: the American-English method, in which the working yarn is held in the knitter's right hand.

Holding the Yarn Experiment with the way you hold the yarn. Weave the yarn through your fingers as shown below, or try other ways until you find a method that works for you. The ability to tension the yarn as it flows through your fingers while knitting will allow you to maintain your gauge and work neat, even stitches. As you become comfortable with it, you'll also see that it's less tiring on the hands.

Knit Stitch The knit stitch is the most common and

Holding the Yarn

versatile stitch of all. It is smooth on one side and bumpy on the other. The smooth side of the knit stitch is generally used as the right side of the work—the side that faces out. The working yarn is always held behind the needle when making the knit stitch. In other words, the knit fabric and the needle will always be between you and the working yarn.

Knitting every row creates garter stitch *(see page 13)* in flat, back-and-forth knitting.

Step 1: Hold the needle with the cast-on stitches in your left hand. The working yarn is already attached to the stitch closest to the needle tip. Holding the empty needle in your right hand, take hold of the working yarn with your right hand, and hold it behind the right needle. Insert the empty needle from front to back through the first stitch on the left needle *(fig. 6a)*. The right needle is behind the left needle.

Step 2: Bring your right hand and forefinger toward the tip of the right needle (the yarn is underneath the right needle). Wrap the yarn around the right needle from back to front *(fig. 6b)*. Be careful not to wrap it around the left needle, too.

Step 3: Keeping the yarn firmly tensioned in your right hand, bring the right needle toward you, pulling a new loop through the old stitch *(fig. 6c)*.

Step 4: With the new stitch on the right needle, slip the old stitch off the left needle *(fig. 6d)*. Unlike the cast-on, the new knit stitches are held on the right needle.

You have just knit your first stitch! Repeat until all the cast-on stitches have been knit and are on the needle held in the right hand.

Knitting the Next Row The second and all subsequent knit rows are worked the same as the first: Knit each stitch on the needle in the left hand.

Step 1: When you have knit all the stitches from the left needle, turn the

KNIT STITCH, AMERICAN-ENGLISH METHOD

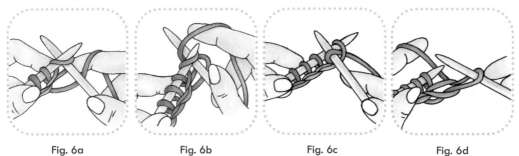

Fig. 6a   Fig. 6b   Fig. 6c   Fig. 6d

work, switching the needle with all the stitches on it from your right hand to your left hand.

Step 2: The working yarn is attached to the stitch closest to the needle tip. Insert the right needle into the first stitch and repeat the knitting steps across the first row, working into each of the stitches of the previous row instead of into the cast-on stitches.

Note: When beginning each new row, be sure the working yarn is *beneath* the needle holding the stitches and is not wrapped over the needle. If the working yarn is pulled upward, the first stitch will appear as two stitches, with both stitch loops appearing in front of the needle. If you knit both loops as single stitches, you'll increase the number of stitches on your needle. Remember, the front loop of each stitch should be in front of the needle and the back loop behind the needle.

Purl Stitch The purl stitch is the reverse of the knit stitch. The yarn is always held in front of the work when making the purl stitch. As you work this stitch, the bumpy side faces you and the side behind the needle is now the smooth side. When working flat, back-and-forth knitting, purling every row creates garter stitch, just the same as knitting every row. Alternating rows of knit and purl makes stockinette stitch, in which the knit side is the right side and the purl side is the wrong side *(see page 13)*. The purl side of stockinette stitch is called reverse stockinette stitch, which uses the purl side as the right side and the knit side as the wrong side.

Step 1: Hold the working yarn and the empty needle in your right hand and the needle with the cast-on stitches in your left hand. With the working yarn held in front of your work, insert the empty needle from right to left through the front loop of the first cast-on stitch *(fig. 7a)*. The right needle is in front of the left needle.

PURL STITCH, AMERICAN-ENGLISH METHOD

Fig. 7a   Fig. 7b   Fig. 7c

Step 2: Bring the yarn in your right hand toward the tip of the right needle. Carry the yarn between the needles, wrapping it around the right needle from top to bottom, ending in front *(fig. 7b)*. Be careful not to wrap it around the left needle.

Step 3: Keeping the working yarn in your right hand, use the right needle to pull up a loop, moving backward and away from you through the stitch on the left needle *(fig. 7c)*. With the new stitch on the right needle, slip the old stitch off the left needle.

Repeat for each new purl stitch.

Purling the Next Row The second and subsequent purl rows are worked the same as the first. Purl each stitch on the needle in the left hand.

Step 1: When you have purled all the stitches from the left needle, turn the work, switching the needle with all the stitches from the right hand to the left.

Step 2: The working yarn is attached to the stitch closest to the needle tip and held in front of the work. Insert the right needle into the first stitch with the yarn held in front of the stitches, and repeat the steps of the first row, working into each of the stitches in the previous row instead of the cast-on stitches.

Binding Off This technique finishes the last row and secures the stitches so the needles can be removed. You will often see the phrase "bind off in pattern." This means work the last row of stitches as instructed, and bind off as you work. It sounds tricky, but it's not. The illustrations below show a knit row for the bind-off, but it's a good idea to practice the technique on both knit and purl rows.

Step 1: Hold the needle with stitches in your left hand and the empty needle in your right hand. Hold the yarn in position for the knit stitch, behind your work.

Step 2: Knit the first 2 stitches.

Step 3: Insert the left needle from left to right into the front loop of the first stitch on the right needle *(fig. 8a)*. **Note:** This is the stitch farther from the right needle tip.

Step 4: Use the left needle to pull this stitch over the second stitch and drop it

BINDING OFF

Fig. 8a

Fig. 8b

Fig. 8c

off the right needle. One stitch is bound off; the second stitch remains on the right needle *(fig. 8b)*.

Step 5: Knit the next stitch.

Step 6: Repeat steps 3–5 until you have bound off all stitches from the left needle and 1 stitch remains on the right needle. Cut the yarn about 4″ (10cm) from the stitch, and pull the yarn tail through the last stitch *(fig. 8c)*. Remove the needle and pull the yarn tail to tighten.

Many new knitters have a tendency to bind off too tightly. The bound-off edge should be as elastic as the rest of the knitting. If necessary, use a larger needle size to work the stitches in your bind-off row.

Basic Stitch Patterns

Garter Stitch Knit every row or purl every row in flat knitting, and you have garter stitch *(fig. 9)*. It's a great stitch pattern for new knitters because it uses only one simple stitch. Because garter stitch lays flat without curling, it's often used at the beginning and end of rows to create flat, noncurling edges. ***Note:*** If you knit in the round, either with circular or

GARTER STITCH

Fig. 9

double-point needles, you'll create stockinette stitch instead of garter stitch.

Stockinette Stitch This is the most commonly used stitch pattern. Simply knit one row, purl the next, and repeat. Stockinette stitch has a tendency to curl at the edges when not stabilized with other, noncurling, stitch patterns, such as garter stitch. Because of that, border stitch patterns are usually added to the lower and upper edges, and the side edges are sewn into the seam.

The knit side (the smooth side) is called stockinette stitch *(fig. 10a)*, and the purl side (bumpy side) is called reverse stockinette stitch *(fig. 10b)*. Reverse stockinette stitch is often used as a background for cable patterns because it shows off the pattern well.

Ribbing You'll recognize ribbing as the stitch often found at the cuffs and hems of sweaters. It is a very elastic pattern and

STOCKINETTE STITCH (KNIT SIDE)

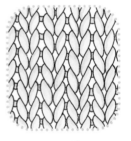

Fig. 10a

REVERSE STOCKINETTE STITCH (PURL SIDE)

Fig. 10b

knits up narrower than stockinette stitch on the same size needles. There are many ways of making ribbing, but the most common are the single rib *(fig. 11a)* and the double rib *(fig. 11b)*. The single rib is made by alternating one knit stitch with one purl stitch. Double rib is more elastic than single rib and is made by alternating two knit stitches with two purl stitches.

The most important thing to remember when making ribbing is that the yarn must be brought between the needles to the back of the work for the knit stitches and between the needles to the front of the work for the purl stitches. If you finish a row and discover extra stitches, or find a hole in the ribbing several rows later, it's probably because you inadvertently knit with the yarn in front or purled with the yarn in back. This can be easily corrected *(see Correcting Mistakes, page 20)*.

Ribbing is easy once you learn to recognize knit and purl stitches. Instead of counting stitches, you'll simply knit the knits and purl the purls.

IS THAT ALL THERE IS TO IT?

You are now a knitter! Practice these basic stitches until you feel comfortable with them, and refer back to the instructions if you get confused.

Use the simple knit and purl stitches to make many wonderful things. But don't stop there! If you keep challenging yourself to try new patterns and learn new techniques, knitting will continue to be an exciting undertaking.

Gauge

The word *gauge* (or *tension*) refers to how many stitches (or rows) there are in an inch of knitting using a specific yarn and needle size. The resulting numbers are used to determine how many stitches and rows it will take to achieve a desired size. Remember, the needle size listed in the pattern is the size the designer used to obtain the listed gauge. Two knitters using the same materials may end up with different gauges. A difference of only half a stitch per inch could make a discrepancy of several inches in the size of the finished project. Take time to make a gauge swatch before starting your project—you'll be glad you did. It may be necessary to make several attempts before you achieve the correct gauge.

SINGLE RIB

Fig. 11a

DOUBLE RIB

Fig. 11b

How to Knit a Gauge Swatch Use the main needle size listed in the pattern. Cast on about 6″ (15cm) of stitches, using the stitch gauge given in the pattern to determine the number to cast on. Work the main pattern until the swatch measures 4″ (10cm) in length; bind off all stitches. Lay the swatch on a flat, hard surface. Measure, then count 4″ (10cm) of stitches across the swatch (*fig. 12a*). Divide this number by 4 to get the number of stitches per inch. Repeat the process a few times in different areas to confirm the count. To measure the rows, center the measuring tape or ruler lengthwise on the swatch, and count the number of rows over 2″ (5cm) (*fig. 12b*) or 4″ (10cm) if the pattern is very large vertically. Divide the total by 2 (or 4, if using that number) to determine the number of rows per inch. *Note:* Knit stitches are wider than they are tall; however, in stitch patterns such as stockinette stitch, you'll normally have more rows per inch than stitches per inch.

Compare your gauge with the pattern gauge. If your gauge swatch has more stitches per inch than the pattern gauge, this means your stitches are smaller than the pattern gauge, and you'll need to try larger needles until your swatch stitches are the same size as the required gauge. If your swatch has fewer stitches per inch than the pattern gauge, your stitches are larger than the pattern gauge, and you'll need to try smaller needles to obtain the pattern gauge. Be exact in your measurements, and knit as many swatches as you need, changing needle sizes until you find the size that allows you to obtain the correct gauge.

Knitting in the Round

To avoid sewing seams, you can work in rounds using circular needles or double-point needles.

Circular Needles To work in rounds, cast your stitches on one end of the needle the same as you would on a straight needle. Check to be sure that the

GAUGE SWATCH

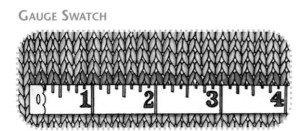

Fig. 12a (20 sitches=4″ [10cm])

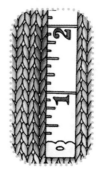

Fig. 12b (12 rows=2″ [5cm])

cast-on lays flat and smooth and is not twisted. Add an open-ring stitch marker to the end of the needle to mark the beginning of the round *(fig. 13a)*, and work the first round according to your pattern instructions.

Double-point Needles Evenly distribute your cast-on among three or four needles, keeping one needle out to knit with. Be sure the cast-on lies flat and smooth and no stitches are twisted. If you'd like, add a stitch marker to the first needle to mark the beginning of the round. (It's easy for a stitch marker to fall off the double-point needle, so keep an eye on it.) The needles either form a triangle (if you cast on to three needles) *(fig. 13b)* or a square (if you cast on to four needles). With the empty needle, knit all stitches on the first needle. When that needle is empty, use it to knit the stitches on the next needle. Continue to knit the stitches from each double-point onto an empty needle, working the stitches as instructed in the pattern.

CIRCULAR NEEDLES   **DOUBLE-POINT NEEDLES**

Fig. 13a   Fig. 13b

Slipping a Stitch

Sometimes instructions tell you to slip a stitch. This means you'll move a stitch to the right needle without knitting or purling. The instructions may indicate whether to slip it as if to knit or purl. **To slip as if to knit** *(fig. 14a)*, keep the yarn behind your work and insert the right needle into the next stitch on the left needle as if to knit it. Simply slide the stitch off the left needle and onto the right. **To slip as if to purl with yarn in back** *(fig. 14b)*, with the knit side facing you, insert the right needle tip into the next stitch on the left needle as if to purl, and slide the stitch onto the right needle. **To slip as if to purl with yarn in front** *(fig. 14c)*, with purl side facing you, slip the stitch as if to purl. When a stitch is slipped using either of these methods, the strand will not show on the knit side of the work. However, some stitch patterns reverse the normal process, so always follow the instructions carefully.

Why does it make a difference how stitches are slipped? When stitches are slipped as if to purl, they are transferred onto the right needle untwisted, which means the front stitch loop remains in front of the needle. When slipped as if to knit, stitches are transferred in a twisted position so the back loop of the stitch is now in front. Some pattern stitches require this.

SLIP STITCH

Fig. 14a

Fig. 14b

Fig. 14c

A rule of thumb about slipping stitches: Always slip as if to purl unless the pattern instructions specify otherwise. An exception to this rule is that you'll always slip as if to knit when the stitch is part of a decrease method. A stitch that's part of a decrease is transferred to the right needle as if to knit, in the twisted position, because it will later become untwisted when the decrease is complete.

Increases

Increases are used to shape your knitting and to create lace patterns. There are many ways to make an increase; we've listed a few standard methods. Many pattern instructions specify which type of increase to use; others do not. It's important to learn how each increase affects the appearance of your work so you can use the appropriate method. Make small knit swatches and practice each increase method listed here. Label them, and keep them for future reference. Avoid making increases and decreases in the edge stitches, because they affect the ability to make a smooth seam when finishing. Make increases or decreases at least one stitch in from the edge stitches.

Yarn Over A yarn over is the basis for most lace patterns and is very simple to make. In fact, many new knitters make yarn overs by accident (but in those cases it's called a hole, not lace). When moving the yarn from the front or the back of your work, you would normally be very careful to put the yarn between the needles and not over one (which would create an extra loop on the needle). To make a yarn over when knitting, bring the yarn to the front of the work and then knit the next stitches as instructed *(fig. 15)*. On the next row, work into the front loop of this strand (yarn over) as you would any

YARN OVER

Fig. 15

KNIT 1 IN THE FRONT AND BACK LOOPS

Fig. 16a

Fig. 16b

other stitch, transferring it from the left needle after it is knitted.

Knit 1 in the Front and Back Loops/ Bar Increase This is one of the most visible increases in stockinette stitch: It leaves a little bump that looks like a purl stitch. Use it decoratively or when the purl bump is part of a stitch pattern. The bar increase is one of the easiest to make. To make it, knit the front loop, but don't remove the stitch from the left needle (fig. 16a). Knit into the back loop of the same stitch (fig.16b).

Make One These increases are made simply by knitting into the horizontal strand between stitches on the right and left needles. One method creates a left-leaning increase, meaning that the front strand of the increase slants to the left. The other method leans to the right. These are called paired increases.

To make a left-leaning increase:

Step 1: Insert the left needle from front to back under the strand (*fig. 17a*).

Step 2: With the right needle, knit into the back of the strand (*fig. 17b*).

Step 3: Slip the strand off the left needle. You now have one new stitch (an increase) on the right needle. Note how the front strand of this new stitch leans toward the left (*fig. 17c*).

To make a right-leaning increase:

Step 1: Insert the left needle from back to front under the strand (*fig. 18a*).

Step 2: Knit into the front of the strand (*fig. 18b*).

Step 3: Slip the strand off the left needle. You now have one new stitch (an increase) on the right needle. Note how the front strand leans toward the right (*fig. 18c*).

MAKE 1 (LEFT-LEANING)

Fig. 17a

Fig. 17b

Fig. 17c

MAKE 1 (RIGHT-LEANING)

Fig. 18a

Fig. 18b

Fig. 18c

Decreases

Use decreases for shaping necklines, making lace patterns, and more. Some decreases have a definite slant either left or right; pattern instructions may specify which type to use. Left- and right-slant decreases are referred to as paired decreases.

Knit Two Together The knit-two-together decrease is made by working into two stitches at the same time. With the yarn behind your work, skip the first stitch on the left needle and insert the right needle knitwise into the second stitch and the first stitch at the same time, knit the two stitches as if they were one stitch (fig. 19), and remove the stitches from the left needle. This decrease leans to the right on the knit side of the work.

KNIT TWO TOGETHER

Fig. 19

Purl Two Together As the name suggests, this decrease is the purl-side method of the knit-two-together increase. With the yarn in front of your work, insert the right needle through the loops of the next two stitches on the left needle as if to purl (fig. 20), purl the two stitches as if they were one stitch, and remove them from the left needle. This decrease leans to the right when it is viewed from the knit side of the work.

PURL TWO TOGETHER

Fig. 20

Slip Slip Knit The slip-slip-knit method is a one-stitch decrease that leans to the left and is usually paired with knit two together on knit rows.

Work this decrease as follows: Slip two stitches knitwise, one at a time, from the left needle onto the right needle; insert the

SLIP SLIP KNIT

Fig. 21

left needle tip from left to right into the front loops of both slipped stitches *(fig. 21)* with the yarn in back, knit both stitches together from this position.

Slip Slip Purl The slip-slip-purl method is a one-stitch decrease made on purl (wrong-side) rows. When viewed from the right side of the work it leans to the left and matches the slip slip knit which is made on knit (right-side) rows. The slip slip purl is usually paired with purl two together on wrong-side rows.

Work this decrease as follows: Slip two stitches knitwise, one at a time, from the left needle onto the right needle (the base of both stitches will be twisted at this point), and slip both stitches back to the left needle in their twisted position *(fig. 22a)*, insert the right needle tip through the back loops of

SLIP SLIP PURL

Fig. 22a

Fig. 22b

both stitches, entering the second stitch first and then the first stitch, and purl them together from this position *(fig. 22b)*.

IMPORTANT THINGS TO KNOW

You've learned the basics of knitting—but there's always more to learn. This section helps you polish your skills so that your projects have a professional look.

Correcting Mistakes

One thing to know about mistakes in knitting is that we *all* make them. Fortunately, knitting is easily corrected, and you'll learn from any missteps along the way. Once you learn to correct them, you'll be happily on your way again.

Dropped Stitches It's a good idea to count your stitches often as you work, especially after casting on and after making increases or decreases. This habit will help you catch many mistakes. If your stitch count is less than it should be, it may be because a stitch has dropped from your needle.

Use a crochet hook to correct a dropped stitch, whether it has dropped one row or several rows (a running stitch).

Step 1: Hold the knit side of the work toward you. Count the horizontal strands between the two needles to determine how many rows the stitch has slipped. It's important to begin with the very first strand closest to the dropped stitch. With the loose horizontal strands

DROPPED STITCHES

Fig. 23a

Fig. 23b

behind the loop of the dropped stitch, insert a crochet hook into the loop from front to back. Catch the first horizontal strand and pull it through the stitch (*fig. 23a*). Repeat the step with each horizontal strand until the dropped stitch is back at the current row.

Step 2: Place the stitch on the left needle *untwisted*, with the right loop of the stitch in front of the needle (*fig. 23b*).

Continue in pattern.

Joining New Yarn

When you near the end of a ball of yarn, try to change to the new yarn at the row edge. This will prevent the stitches in the middle of your work from becoming uneven, and it will make weaving in the yarn tails much easier, because you can hide them in the seams.

Step 1: Using an overhand knot (to be removed when finishing the item), tie the old and new yarns together close to the needle, leaving a 4–6″ (10–15cm) tail on both yarns.

Step 2: Drop the old yarn, and begin knitting with the new one. Once you are more experienced and feel more comfortable with controlling the yarns, you may choose to omit knotting the yarns together and simply drop the old yarn and start knitting with the new strand, tightening and securing the yarn tails later.

Another option is to hold the old and new yarn together and knit with both for a few stitches. Then drop the old yarn and continue with the new. This method attaches the yarn securely and decreases the number of ends to weave in later, but it can leave a noticeable lump, so don't use it in a prominent place.

Changing Colors When changing colors somewhere other than the end of a row, drop the old color on the wrong side, pick up the new color from underneath the old, and continue knitting with the new color (*fig. 24*). This prevents a hole from appearing between colors.

Intarsia Knitting In intarsia knitting the pattern is worked in large blocks of color at a time, and the stitches in each color area are worked from their own yarn supply. Even though intarsia often uses many

CHANGING COLORS

Fig. 24

different colors, it produces a single-layer fabric. In each row, when each group of stitches in one color is completed, that color is dropped (don't cut the yarn) and the next color group of stitches is worked from its own yarn source, either from small individual balls of color that are joined to the work at specific sections or by winding yarn onto bobbins. Always drop the old color on the wrong side, pick up the new color from underneath the old, and continue knitting with the new color.

Making an I-Cord

You can make an I-cord to use as a drawstring, strap, or tie using double-point needles or a short circular needle. **Step 1:** Cast on 3 or 4 stitches to one double-point needle. Slide the stitches to the other end of the needle. The working yarn is at the "wrong" end of the needle *(fig. 25a)*. **Step 2:** With the yarn strand across the back of the stitches, pull it up to the front at the needle tip and knit the stitches *(fig. 25b)*. **Step 3**: Repeat step 2 until the cord is the desired length. Unless instructed

I-CORD

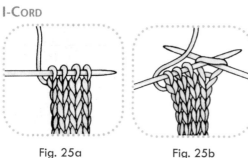

Fig. 25a   Fig. 25b

otherwise, finish the last row as slip 1, knit 2 together, pass the slipped stitch over. Cut the yarn, and thread the end through the last stitch.

FINISHING

Most knitters prefer knitting to sewing seams and weaving in ends, but taking care with these final steps ensures that your knitting is shown at its best on both the outside and the inside.

Picking Up Stitches

Pick up stitches using a knitting needle or crochet hook. For a neater edge, use needles or a hook one or two sizes smaller than the working needle. After the pickup is finished, change to the needle size indicated in the instructions. Work with the right side of the piece facing you, unless instructed otherwise. Divide the area of pickup into quarter sections, or smaller spaces if necessary, and mark with pins or thread. This will help you maintain the same number of stitches in each. Example: Pick up and knit 100 stitches. Divide the area into fourths, and pick up 25 stitches in each quarter section. If the border uses a different color from the pickup area, pick up the stitches in the main color, then change to the new color on the next row.

Picking Up Stitches Along a Bound-off Edge With the right side of the garment facing you, insert the tip of the right needle into the first full stitch beneath the bind-off row (fig. 26a), wrap the yarn around the needle, and pull it through the stitch, creating a new stitch on the needle. Repeat for each stitch until the required number of stitches are on the needle.

Picking Up Stitches Along a Side Edge With the right side facing you, unless instructed otherwise, join the working yarn at the lower edge if not already attached (see Joining New Yarn, page 21). Insert the right needle into the fabric through the first full stitch of the first row, and wrap the yarn around the needle knitwise. Pull through a loop, creating a new stitch on the right needle (fig. 26b). Repeat the process, spacing the pickup stitches along the side edge as necessary, but always working into a full stitch. It's important not to leave any holes or uneven spaces in the work.

Picking Up Stitches Along a Curved Edge Curved edges are usually a combination of edges—horizontal, diagonal, and vertical. To pick up stitches along an edge that was formed by making decreases, such as along the neck shaping of a sweater, insert the needle into the stitch below the edge stitch (fig. 26c)—not between the stitches—to prevent holes from occurring when the pickup is finished.

Sewing Seams

While it may be tempting to hurry through the finishing so you can finally see the completed project, it's important not to rush through sewing the seams if you want the end result to look polished and professional. Block each piece before assembling (see Washing and Blocking, page 32), and allow the pieces to dry. This helps the edges remain flat as you work.

Picking Up Stitches

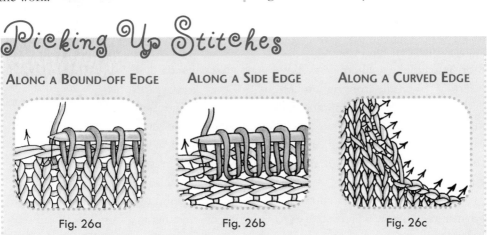

ALONG A BOUND-OFF EDGE   **ALONG A SIDE EDGE**   **ALONG A CURVED EDGE**

Fig. 26a   Fig. 26b   Fig. 26c

Shoulder Seams (bound-off edge)

Step 1: Lay both pieces flat, with right sides up. Thread a tapestry needle, and, beginning at the right-side edge of the piece closest to you (the lower piece), insert the needle from back to front through the center of the first stitch. Pull the yarn through, leaving a yarn tail to weave in later.

SHOULDER SEAMS

Fig. 27

Step 2: Insert the needle from right to left under the two vertical legs of the first stitch on the piece farther from you *(fig. 27)*, then insert the needle from right to left under the next two vertical legs on the near piece, beginning in the same hole as the first stitch made. Pull the yarn gently to adjust the stitch and close the stitches together.

Step 3: Continue to alternate sides, inserting the needle from right to left under two strands and beginning in the same hole as the last stitch made. Pull the yarn every few stitches to adjust it and close the seam. At the end of the seam, weave in the yarn tail.

Mattress Stitch Mattress stitch is a great stitch to know when it comes to sewing vertical seams, including side and sleeve seams.

Step 1: Thread a tapestry needle with matching yarn, leaving a 4″ (10cm) tail to weave in later. With both pieces flat and right sides up, insert the needle under the horizontal strand between the first and second stitches of the first row on one piece and the corresponding strand on the second piece. Gently pull the yarn to tighten.

Step 2: Insert the needle under the horizontal strand on the next row of one piece, and then insert the needle under the strand on the same row of the other piece.

Step 3: Continue to work under the horizontal strands, alternating pieces, until you have six to eight rows worked *(fig. 28)*, and then pull the yarn gently to close the seam.

Step 4: Continue weaving together to the end of the seam. Weave yarn tails into the seam stitches, and secure.

MATTRESS STITCH

Fig. 28

Whipstitch This illustration shows whipstitch made on flat fabric as a decorative false seam *(fig. 29)*. The same method is also used to actually join two pieces together in a seam, which can be

WHIPSTITCH

Fig. 29

BACKSTITCH

Fig. 30

made on the wrong side of the work, or on the right side to create a sporty look.

To work flat: With threaded tapestry needle, bring the needle to the front surface *(position 1),* move the needle upward and to the left of the entry point, insert the needle to the back of the fabric *(position 2),* exit the fabric to the front *(position 3);* repeat 2 and 3 until the decoration or seam is finished. Take the yarn to the wrong side of the work and weave it through several stitches to secure.

To seam edge stitches: Align both pieces of fabric with the edges to be seamed next to each other. Insert a threaded tapestry needle from back to front through both edge stitches *(position 1),* draw yarn through; *move the needle to the left of the first two stitches joined and insert needle from back to front through the next set of edge stitches *(positions 2 and 3);* repeat from * until all stitches are joined and seam is closed.

Backstitch Backstitch is an easy way to make a firm seam.

Step 1: Thread a tapestry needle with matching yarn. With the right sides together, work along the wrong sides about one stitch in from the edges. Work two running stitches on top of each other to secure the lower edges.

Step 2: With the tapestry needle and yarn behind the work, insert the needle through both layers of fabric about two stitches to the left of the running stitch and pull the yarn to the front of the work.

Step 3: Insert the needle from front to back one stitch back to the right, working through both layers.

Step 4: Moving forward to the left about two stitches, bring the needle to the front of the work, about one stitch ahead of the original stitch *(fig. 30).* Repeat the process until you reach the end of the seam, working one stitch backward (to the right) on the front side of the work and two stitches forward (to the left) on the back side of the work.

Step 5: Finish the seam by working two or three running stitches on top of each other, stitching over the bound-off edges. Weave in yarn tails.

Invisible Seam on Garter Stitch As its name suggests, this seam, which also works on seed-stitch fabrics, disappears into the knitting.

INVISIBLE SEAM ON GARTER STITCH

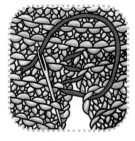

Fig. 31

Align both pieces of fabric together, matching the top and bottom edges. *Insert the threaded tapestry needle under the top loop of the purl stitch on one edge, pull the yarn through, move the needle across to the adjacent piece of fabric and insert the needle under the bottom loop of the purl stitch on this side, pull yarn through; repeat from * working from side to side to the end of seam. Adjust the yarn tension after seaming several stitches so that each side stitch touches, but doesn't overlap, the other *(fig. 31)*. When the seam is finished, weave in the loose ends to wrong side of work.

Three-needle Bind-off This bind-off finishes off two edges, binding off the stitches and closing the seam at the same time. Normally used to close shoulders,

it can also be used to close side seams when working a garment from side to side. You can also pick up stitches along two side edges and then use the three-needle bind-off to close those seams. To make a flat, neat seam on the right side, follow these instructions:

Step 1: With the right sides of the work together, and with the needle tips aligned and facing to the right *(fig. 32a)*, hold both needles in your left hand.

Step 2: Insert the empty right needle into the first stitch on each of the two needles in the left hand, and knit the two stitches together *(fig. 32b)*. Slip them off the needle as you would a knit stitch. You now have one stitch on the right needle.

Step 3: Knit the next pair of stitches the same way. You now have two stitches on the right needle.

Step 4: Pull the first stitch on the right needle over the second stitch (the one closest to the tip), just as you would in a normal bind-off *(fig. 32c)*.

THREE-NEEDLE BIND-OFF

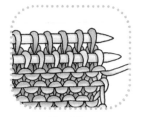

Fig. 32a

Fig. 32b

Fig. 32c

Step 5: Repeat steps 3 and 4 until all stitches have been bound off. Cut the yarn and pull the end through the last loop; weave in the end to secure.

Kitchener Stitch (Grafting) This technique joins live stitches together in an elastic, invisible seam. The method can also be used over bound-off stitches to make a strong, stable seam.

With an equal number of stitches on two needles, and right sides up, hold the needles parallel to each other with points facing right. Thread a blunt tapestry needle with two to three times the length of the area to be joined. For live stitches, work as follows:

Step 1: Insert threaded needle into the first stitch on the front needle purlwise (as if to purl); leave stitch on needle.

Step 2: Insert needle into the first stitch on the back needle knitwise (as if to knit); leave stitch on needle.

Step 3: Insert needle into the same first stitch on the front needle knitwise *(fig. 33a),* slip stitch off needle. Insert needle

into the next front stitch purlwise; leave stitch on needle *(fig. 33b).*

Step 4: Insert needle into the same stitch on the back needle purlwise *(fig. 33c);* slip stitch off needle. Insert needle into the next back stitch knitwise; leave stitch on needle *(fig. 33d).*

Repeat steps 3 and 4 until all stitches are worked.

Tip: To make the technique easier as you work, remember this: Front needle—purlwise leave on, knitwise take off; back needle—knitwise leave on, purlwise take off.

Weaving in Yarn Tails

Carefully weaving in the yarn tails makes your knitting look neat and keeps it from pulling loose and unraveling over time.

Thread a tapestry needle with the yarn tail. Working on the wrong side of the knitting, weave the needle in and out of the back of the stitches for a few inches in one direction, and then turn and work in the opposite direction for an inch or two. Pull the yarn gently to tighten, and

KITCHENER STITCH

Fig. 33a

Fig. 33b

Fig. 33c

Fig. 33d

cut it close to the work. Stretch the knitting slightly so the tail disappears into the last stitch.

Duplicate Stitch

Duplicate stitch is used to create small motifs, make small additions to intarsia, mend socks, and cover knitting errors. It produces a stiff fabric, as stitches are duplicated on top of the knit fabric below. The technique is worked horizontally, vertically, and diagonally.

For horizontal stitches:

Step 1: Thread a tapestry needle with the same yarn type as the knit fabric beneath. Work with strands about 18″ (45.5cm) long to avoid having the yarn plies untwist and fibers shed as the needle is repeatedly drawn through the knit fabric. Rethread the tapestry needle as necessary.

Step 2: Begin the first duplicate stitch in the lower right corner of the motif or pattern. (You'll work from right to left.) Secure the yarn on the wrong side of the fabric, and bring the needle through to the front of the fabric at the base of the first stitch.

Step 3: Insert the needle into the right side of the top of the same stitch, carry the needle and yarn across the back of the work, and bring them to the front on the left side of the same stitch *(fig. 34a).* Reinsert the needle into the base of the first stitch.

Step 4: Bring the needle up through the base of the stitch to the left of the stitch just duplicated. Repeat step 3.

To work the next horizontal row, insert the needle into the base of the last horizontal stitch worked, and then bring needle and yarn out to the front through the center of that stitch. Turn the work (the motif will be upside down), and work horizontal stitches across the second row of motif stitches, working the same as the previous row. Continue working horizontal stitches from right to left on each row. Weave the yarn tails through the backs of stitches to secure.

For vertical stitches, begin at the lowest point and work upward. Work the same as for horizontal duplicate stitch, but bring the needle out to the front through the center of the stitch above the one just worked rather than the stitch to the left *(fig. 34b).*

DUPLICATE STITCH

Fig. 34a   Fig. 34b

Diagonal stitches are made using a combination of horizontal and vertical methods. Work one stitch horizontally, and instead of finishing by moving to the next stitch on the left in the same row, bring the needle out at the base of the next stitch on the left, one row above.

Chain Stitch Embroidery

Chain stitch is a basic embroidery technique often used to embellish knit and crochet projects, as well as fabric. To create flowers, the basic chain stitch is grouped around a center to form petals or attached along a stem to form leaves.

Step 1: Bring threaded needle to the front of the fabric at the first flower petal position. The needle should be at the flower's center, not the outer edges.

Step 2: Move the needle over 1 or 2 threads, insert it to the back of the fabric and back through to the front again at the desired petal length with thread under the needle.

Step 3: Insert needle to back again, catching the flower petal loop as shown *(fig. 35a),* move the needle upward and to the left, and exit to the front at the position for the next petal.

Repeat steps 2 and 3 for as many petals as needed *(fig. 35b).* After the last petal is finished, take yarn to back and secure the thread by weaving it through several stitches.

Making Pom-poms

Cut 2 circles out of cardboard, each about 1½″ (4cm) in diameter. Cut a small hole in the center of each circle; make a slit from outside edge of both circles to the center hole. Hold both circles together with slits aligned. Wind yarn evenly around both circles (going through the slits to the center holes) as tightly as possible. The more times you wrap, the fuller the pom-pom. Cut yarn around outer edges of circles. Cut an 18″ (45.5cm) yarn strand, and pulling cardboard circles apart very slightly, wrap strand yarn firmly around pom-pom center a couple of times. Tie strand tightly in a double knot. Remove cardboard circles completely, and fluff out pom-pom. Trim ends to even out if necessary, but do not trim yarn around pom-pom centers. You will use these to attach the pom-pom to your project.

CHAIN STITCH EMBROIDERY

Fig. 35a   Fig. 35b

Crochet

Knowing how to work a few basic crochet stitches is very useful in knitting. Chain stitch and single crochet are frequently used by knitters to create decorative edges, to cast on or bind off, and to make button-holes, buttons, accessory cords, embellishments, and more. Hook sizes are coordinated with knitting needle sizes, but the system for labeling size is different. Crochet hooks are numbered in several different ways. The smallest sizes are steel hooks, which use numbers. The higher the number, the smaller the hook size. Larger hooks are labeled with letters and numbers, A/0 through P/16. Some brands also include metric sizes. Many knitters use a hook one or two sizes smaller than their needle size to prevent the crochet from becoming ruffled or wavy instead of lying flat and smooth against the knit fabric. Practice on your gauge swatch to determine which size hook works best for your project.

Crochet Chain The chain stitch forms the foundation row in crochet. It is quick and easy to make.

Step 1: Begin with a slipknot. Insert the crochet hook into the center of the slipknot from right to left, catching the working yarn (*fig. 36a*). Pull up a loop, and place it on the crochet hook. Pull both the yarn tail and the working yarn to make the slipknot snug around the shank of the crochet hook.

Step 2: Holding the hook in your right hand and the working yarn in your left, bring the yarn over the hook from back to front, and pull it through the loop on the crochet hook (*fig. 36b*).

Step 3: Repeat step 2 until the chain is the desired length. When the last chain loop is made, cut the working yarn, leaving a tail to weave in later.

Step 4: Thread the tail through the last chain loop on the hook, and pull to tighten and secure.

Single Crochet Single crochet can be used as a quick and easy finishing edge on your knitted pieces. It is attached either directly to knit stitches, along a bound-off edge, or as a border for other crochet stitches. It makes a firm finish and helps the edges lay flat.

CROCHET CHAIN

Fig. 36a

Fig. 36b

SINGLE CROCHET

Fig. 37a

Fig. 37b

Fig. 37c

Step 1: Insert the hook under a bound-off stitch (or where directed in the instructions). Bring the working yarn over the hook and pull through a loop, yarn over again, and pull it through the loop on the hook *(fig. 37a)*.

Step 2: Insert the hook under the next bound-off stitch *(fig. 37b)*, yarn over, and pull up a loop (two loops on hook). Yarn over again, and pull the yarn back through both loops on the hook *(fig. 37c)*, leaving one loop on the hook.

Step 3: Repeat step 2 until the required number of stitches is complete. Finish according to pattern instructions.

Double Crochet This stitch is worked into a chain, single crochet, or directly into the knitting, as shown below.

Step 1: Insert the hook into the knitting one stitch in from the edge, yarn over, and pull up a loop. Yarn over again, and pull it through the loop on the hook. Yarn over, insert the hook into the next base stitch *(fig. 38a)*, and pull up a loop (three loops on hook). Yarn over and pull it through the first two loops *(fig. 38b)*, yarn over, and pull it through the last two loops *(fig. 38c)*.

The double crochet is complete; one loop is on the hook *(fig. 38d)*.

DOUBLE CROCHET

Fig. 38a

Fig. 38b

Fig. 38c

Fig. 38d

Step 2: Yarn over, insert the hook in the next stitch, yarn over, and pull up a loop (three loops on hook). Yarn over and pull it through two loops, yarn over and pull it through the remaining two loops. The second double crochet is complete, with one loop left on the hook.

Repeat step 2 for pattern. To end the last stitch, after completing step 2, cut the yarn and pull it through the last loop on the hook.

Washing and Blocking

Always save at least one label from your yarn when you make an item that needs to be washed often. Keep it where you can easily find it. Some yarns can be safely washed in the washing machine and dried in the dryer; others cannot. If you have any doubt, play it safe—hand wash it.

Fill a sink with lukewarm water (never hot!), and add a small amount of mild soap for delicate knits. Put the garment in the sink, and allow it to soak. Do not agitate or handle roughly. Drain the sink, and gently press down on the garment to squeeze out some of the water. Never wring or twist a wet item; always support the weight so the item doesn't stretch. Fill the sink with cool rinse water; allow the item to soak, drain the water, and again gently press out the excess water. Repeat until the soap is removed.

Spread a layer of thick towels on a flat surface. (Never hang a knitted garment.) Lift the garment from the sink with both hands without stretching it, and spread it out on the prepared surface. Use a tape measure to shape it to the correct measurements. Pin in place using rustproof T-pins, and let dry.

Some yarns, including wool, can be blocked by using steam, but always check the yarn label first. Lay the garment on a blocking board, and pin it to the correct measurements. Keep the steam spray several inches above the garment—never spray it directly onto the garment.

Felting

Felting is the process of using hot water, agitation, and suds to change (or shrink) a knitted piece into a felted fabric that will not unravel, even when cut. Felting creates a very durable fabric that is practical as well as beautiful.

When making an item to be felted, use extra-large needles and make it several sizes larger than normal. This creates space between the stitches and rows and allows the fibers to shrink while maintaining a smooth fabric surface.

Animal fibers are best for felting. You can use wool, mohair, camel, and alpaca, among others. Superwash wool yarns have been treated to resist shrinking—they will not felt. Synthetic yarns do not felt, either.

To felt, set the washing machine on the hot water cycle and low water level. Add a small amount of dishwashing liquid; too many suds hampers the felting process. Add towels, tennis balls, or washable sneakers to the machine to balance the load and aid the felting process. Allow the machine to agitate for five minutes, then stop it to check the amount of felting. Continue to check every five minutes or so until the stitches completely disappear and the item is the desired size. The amount of felting time varies depending upon the yarn, washing machine, and hardness of water.

Once the desired felting stage is obtained, remove the item from the washing machine, drain the soapy water, and fill it with cold rinse water. Soak the item in rinse water for several minutes to remove all soapiness. Set the machine directly on spin cycle to eliminate excess water from the felted item, or wrap it in a large towel and squeeze to take out the rinse water. Remove the felted item from the machine immediately after spinning to avoid wrinkling the fabric. Stretch, pull, and pat it into shape, and allow it to air-dry on a flat surface.

Understanding Knitting Instructions

Like most crafts, knitting has its own language. Knitting patterns use abbreviations, special terms, and punctuation. The language may seem strange at first, but you will quickly master it and be reading patterns like a pro.

Read any special notes or instructions for the pattern you plan to make. When a "finished size" is listed, the numbers given refer to the garment size upon completion (provided you maintain the correct gauge).

Reading through the entire pattern may be confusing at first, so study small sections. Pay attention to punctuation. One sentence usually represents one row; commas and semicolons may mean that something's going to change with the next stitch or row. Instructions inside asterisks, brackets, or parentheses are usually repeated, so look for the directions that explain what to do.

Schematics These are line drawings of the basic garment pieces, to which measurements are added. Usually schematics show the basic measurements before neck ribbing, collars, or other embellishments are added. Check the schematic to determine which size will best fit you in width and length.

Sunny Baby Blanket

Of course this blanket can be knit in any color you please, but bright yellow brings an extra spark of joy and light. A pretty textured pattern makes it even livelier. The more you wash this yarn, the softer it gets.

Designer: Lucie Sinkler

Size

30½×34″ (77.5×86.5cm)

What You'll Need

Yarn: Machine-washable worsted weight yarn, about 800 yards (731.5m)

We used: Plymouth Encore (75% acrylic, 25% wool; 200 yards [183m] per 3½oz [100g] skein): #215, 4 skeins

Needles: US size 8 (5mm) circular, 29″ (73.5cm) long

Notion: Tapestry needle to weave in ends

Gauge

17 stitches and 32 rows=4″ (10cm) in garter stitch (knit every row)

Make the blanket

Cast on 132 stitches.

Rows 1–16: Knit.

Begin pattern:

Row 1 (right side): Knit.

Row 2 (wrong side): Knit 8, (purl 8, knit 4) 9 times, purl 8, knit 8.

Rows 3, 5, 7, 9, and 11: Repeat row 1.

Rows 4, 6, 8, 10, and 12: Repeat row 2.

Rows 13–18: Knit.

Repeat pattern (rows 1–18) 11 times more. Repeat rows 1–12 once more. Knit 16 rows for border.

Bind off, and weave loose ends to wrong side of work. Wash and block.

Fuzzy-Fringe Sweater and Hat

If you want to knit a sweater but are leery of complicated shaping patterns, look no further! This great-looking sweater (and equally adorable hat) is knit entirely in rectangular sections and then seamed together—no shaping required!

Designer: Lesley Edmondson

Size

6–12 months

Sweater
Chest: 26″ (66cm)
Length: 9″ (23cm)

Hat
Circumference: 13″ (33cm)

What You'll Need

Yarn: Worsted weight yarn, approximately 600 yards (548.5m); novelty eyelash yarn, about 60 yards (55m)

We used: Karabella Aurora 8 (100% merino wool; 98 yards [90m] per 50g ball): #1536 Pistachio (yarn A), 6 balls; Crystal Palace Fizz (100% polyester; 120 yards [110m] per 50g ball): #7312 Lettuce (yarn B), 1 ball

Needles: US size 7 (4.5mm)

Notions: Long sewing pins; tapestry needle; sewing needle and matching thread; 6 decorative buttons, about ½″ (1.3cm) diameter each

Gauge

18 stitches and 36 rows=4″ (10cm)

Make the sweater

Back

With 1 strand each of yarns A and B held together as 1, cast on 60 stitches and work in garter stitch (knit every row) for 6 rows. Cut yarn B leaving 4″ (10cm) tail, and work even with yarn A in garter stitch until piece measures 9″ (23cm) from cast-on edge. Bind off.

Front panel (make 2)

With 1 strand each of yarns A and B held together as 1, cast on 30 stitches and work in garter stitch (knit every row) for 6 rows. Cut yarn B leaving 4″ (10cm) tail, and work even with yarn A in garter stitch until piece measures 9″ (23cm) from cast-on edge. Bind off.

Sleeves (make 2)

With 1 strand each of yarns A and B held together as 1, cast on 40 stitches and work in garter stitch (knit every row) for 6 rows. Cut yarn B leaving 4″ (10cm) tail, and work even with yarn A in garter stitch until piece measures 6½″ (16.5cm) from cast-on edge. Bind off.

Finishing

Shoulder seams: With right sides together, pin 1 front panel and back piece together from armhole edge to neck. With yarn A threaded on tapestry needle, and beginning at armhole edge, backstitch shoulders together ending seam about 1½" (4cm) from center front. (You will fold back the rest of the center front edge at neck to form lapels.) Repeat shoulder seam on other half of sweater.

Sleeve seams: Fold 1 sleeve in half with right sides together. Match fold to shoulder seam, and pin in place. Smooth each side of sleeve top along the center armhole edges and pin to sweater. Repeat for second sleeve. Turn sweater right side out. Join side seams below sleeves using yarn A and mattress stitch for garter stitch. Join sleeve seams with yarn A and mattress stitch for garter stitch.

Fold back about 1½" (4cm) at the neck edge of each front panel to form lapels, sew them securely in place at the corners using needle and thread. Weave in loose ends. Sew decorative buttons to front of sweater. (***Note:*** Small buttons may pose a choking hazard, so stitch to the sweater securely and check after washing.) Block.

Make the hat

With 1 strand each of yarns A and B held together as 1, cast on 60 stitches and work in garter stitch (knit every row) for 6 rows.

Cut B leaving 4" (10cm) tail, work even in garter stitch with A until piece measures 5½" (14cm) from cast-on edge. Bind off.

Finishing

Fold hat piece in half so short ends meet and wrong sides are together. With yarn A threaded on tapestry needle and using mattress stitch for garter stitch, seam these edges together. Turn work so seam is in the back, and stitch across the bound-off edges using whipstitch to close the top of hat.

Shape corner edges: Turn hat to wrong side. With yarn A threaded on tapestry needle, backstitch a short diagonal "seam" across each corner edge, beginning about 12 rows (6 garter ridges) down from top of hat and ending about 6 stitches in from the top sides. Turn hat right side out. Weave in all ends to wrong side of hat. Sew decorative buttons securely to front of hat.

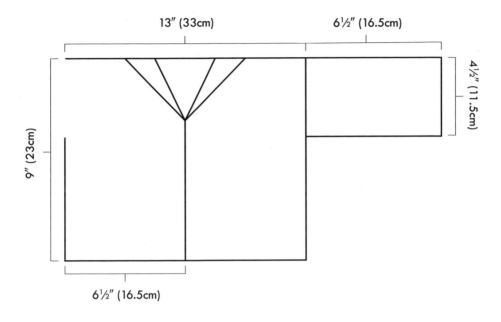

13" (33cm) 6½" (16.5cm)

4½" (11.5cm)

9" (23cm)

6½" (16.5cm)

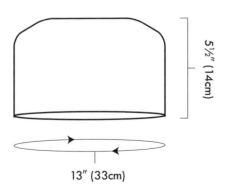

5½" (14cm)

13" (33cm)

Lacy Tank Dress

This is the sweetest little dress, with a lacy skirt and cute tank-style top. Its simple and delicate shape will look gorgeous on your favorite princess.

Designer: Beth Walker-O'Brien

Size

0–6 months: chest 18½" (47cm), length 17" (43cm)

6–12 months: chest 21" (53.5cm), length 18" (45.5cm)

2 years: chest 23¼" (59cm), length 20" (51cm)

3 years: chest 25½" (65cm), length 21" (53.5cm)

What You'll Need

Yarn: DK weight yarn, about 548 [548, 685, 685] yards (500m [500m, 625m, 625m])

We used: Plymouth Yarns Wildflower DK (51% cotton, 49% acrylic; 137 yards [125m] per 50g skein): #53 Light Pink, 4 [4, 5, 5] skeins

Needles: US size 5 (3.75mm); US size 7 (4.5mm)

Notions: 4 stitch holders; tapestry needle

Gauge

24 stitches and 26 rows=4" (10cm) in stockinette stitch

Note: Instructions are given for smallest size; numbers for larger sizes are in brackets. When only 1 number is given, it applies to all sizes.

Ridged Feather Stitch

Row 1 (wrong side): Purl.
Row 2: Knit.
Row 3: Purl.
Row 4: Knit 1, (purl 2 together) 2 times, *(yarn over, knit 1) 3 times, yarn over, (purl 2 together) 4 times; repeat from * until 5 stitches remain, (purl 2 together) 2 times, knit 1.

Make the dress

Back

With size 5 (3.75mm) needle cast on 90 [101, 112, 123] stitches.

Next row (right-side set-up row): Purl.

Change to size 7 (4.5mm) needles and work Ridged Feather Stitch pattern beginning with row 1 (purl row) until piece measures approximately 9" [9½", 10½", 11"] (23cm [24cm, 26.5cm, 28cm]) ending with row 3 (wrong side).

Next row (decrease row): Knit 1, (purl 2 together) 2 times, *purl 3, (purl 2 together) 4 times; repeat from * until 1 stitch remains, knit 1. (58 [65, 72, 79] stitches)

Work even in stockinette stitch (knit on right side, purl on wrong side) until piece measures 4" [4", 4½", 4½"] (10cm [10cm,

11.5cm, 11.5cm]) from beginning of stockinette stitch, ending with a wrong-side row.

Shape armhole

Note: In the following rows of armhole shaping, binding off of armhole edge stitches is worked on right-side and wrong-side rows. Decreases are worked on right-side rows only.

Continue in stockinette stitch, binding off 4 stitches at beginning of each armhole edge 0 [0, 1, 1] time(s). (58 [65, 64, 71] stitches)

Bind off 3 stitches at beginning of each armhole edge 1 [2, 1, 2] time(s). (52 [53, 58, 59] stitches)

Bind off 2 stitches at beginning of each armhole edge 1 [1, 2, 2] time(s). (48 [49, 50, 51] stitches)

Next right-side row: Knit 1, work slip slip knit decrease, knit across row to last 3 stitches, knit 2 together, knit 1. (46 [47, 48, 49] stitches)
Next wrong-side row: Purl.

Repeat last 2 rows 3 [2, 1, 0] time(s) more. (40 [43, 46 49] stitches)

Work even in stockinette stitch until piece measures 6½″ [7″, 7½″, 8″] (16.5cm [18cm, 19cm, 20.5cm]) from beginning of stockinette stitch, ending with a wrong-side row.

Next row (right side): Knit 13 [14, 15, 16] stitches, bind off next 14 [15, 16, 17] stitches, knit to end. (13 [14, 15, 16] stitches on each side of neck edge)

Shape left side of neck (as worn)

Note: In the following left-side neckline shaping rows, binding off of neckline stitches occurs on right-side rows only beginning at neck edge. On wrong-side rows all stitches are purled. Decreases are made on right-side rows at the neck edge.

Continue in stockinette stitch.
Next row and all wrong-side rows: Purl.
Right-side rows: Bind off 3 stitches at neck edge 0 [0, 1, 1] time(s). (13 [14, 12, 13] stitches)

Right-side rows: Bind off 2 stitches at neck edge 1 [2, 1, 2] time(s) more. (11 [10, 10, 9] stitches)

Next row (right side): Knit 1, work slip slip knit decrease, work to end of row. (10 [9, 9, 8] stitches)

Next row: Purl.

Repeat last 2 rows 2 [1, 1, 0] time(s) more. (8 stitches)

Work even until piece measures 17″ [18″, 20″, 21″] (43cm [45.5cm, 51cm, 53.5cm]) from cast-on edge. Place 8 remaining shoulder stitches on holder.

Shape right side of neck (as worn)
Note: In the following right-side neckline shaping rows, binding off of stitches occurs on wrong-side rows only beginning at neck edge. On right-side rows all stitches are knit. Decreases are made on right-side rows at the neck edge.

With wrong side facing, join new yarn and continue in stockinette stitch binding off 3 stitches at neck edge 0 [0, 1, 1] time(s), purl to end of row. (13 [12, 12, 13] stitches)

Next row and all right-side rows: Knit.
Wrong-side rows: Bind off 2 stitches at neck edge 1 [2, 1, 2] time(s). (11 [10, 10, 9] stitches)

Next row (right side): Knit to last 3 stitches, knit 2 together, knit 1. (10 [9, 9, 8] stitches)

Next row (wrong side): Purl.

Repeat last 2 rows 2 [1, 1, 0] time(s) more. (8 stitches)

Work even until piece measures 17″ [18″, 20″, 21″] (43cm [45.5cm, 51cm, 53.5cm]) from cast-on edge. Place 8 shoulder stitches on holder.

Front
Follow instructions for back through armhole shaping until piece measures 5½″ [6″, 6½″, 7″] (14cm [15cm, 16.5cm, 18cm]) from beginning of stockinette stitch, ending with a wrong-side row. (40 [43, 46, 49] stitches)

Next row (right side): Knit 16 [17, 18, 19] stitches, bind off 8 [9, 10, 11] stitches, knit to end of row. (16 [17, 18, 19] stitches each side of neck)

Shape right side of neck (as worn)
Next row and all wrong-side rows: Purl.
Right-side rows: Bind off 3 stitches at neck edge 1 [1, 2, 2] time(s). (13 [14, 12, 13] stitches)

Right-side rows: Bind off 2 stitches at neck edge 1 [2, 1, 2] time(s). (11 [10, 10, 9] stitches)

Next right-side row: Knit 1, work slip slip knit decrease, knit to end of row. (10 [9, 9, 8] stitches)

Next row (wrong-side): Purl.

Repeat last 2 rows 2 [1, 1, 0] time(s) more. (8 stitches)

Work even until piece measures 17″ [18″, 20″, 21″] (43cm [45.5cm, 51cm, 53.5cm]) from cast-on edge. Place 8 shoulder stitches on holder.

Shape left side of neck (as worn)

Continue in stockinette stitch, with wrong side of work facing, join new yarn, bind off 3 stitches at neck edge 1 [1, 2, 2] time(s), purl to end of row. (13 [14, 12, 13] stitches)

All right-side rows: Knit.

Wrong-side rows: Bind off 2 stitches at neck edge 1 [2, 1, 2] time(s), purl to end of row. (10 [9, 9, 8] stitches)

Next right-side row: Knit to last 3 stitches, knit 2 together, knit 1. (10 [9, 9, 8] stitches)

Next wrong-side row: Purl.

Repeat these 2 rows 2 [1, 1, 0] time(s) more. (8 stitches)

Work even until piece measures 17″ [18″, 20″, 21″] (43cm [45.5cm, 51cm, 53.5cm]). Place 8 shoulder stitches on holder.

Finishing

With wrong sides facing (right sides together), seam left shoulder stitches of front and back together using 3-needle bind-off technique.

Work left armhole band

With size 5 (3.75mm) needle and right side facing, pick up 64 [68, 76, 88] stitches around armhole edge starting at bottom of armhole of back piece.

Knit 4 rows. Bind off loosely.

Work neckband

With size 5 (3.75mm) needle and right side facing, pick up 78 [84, 90, 96] stitches around neck edge starting at right shoulder of front piece.

Knit 4 rows. Bind off loosely.

With wrong sides facing (right sides together), seam right shoulder stitches of front and back together using 3-needle bind-off technique. Seam neckband edges together at right shoulder.

Work right armhole band

With size 5 (3.75mm) needle and right side facing, pick up same number of stitches as left armhole band, starting at bottom of armhole of front piece.

Knit 4 rows. Bind off loosely. With yarn threaded on tapestry needle sew side seams using mattress stitch. Weave in loose ends to wrong side of dress.

7¼" [7¾", 8¼", 8¾"]
(18.5cm [19.5cm, 21cm, 22cm])

3" [3½", 4", 4½"]
(7.5cm [9cm, 10cm, 11cm])

3½" [4", 4½", 5"]
(9cm [10cm, 11cm, 12.5cm])

17" [18", 20", 21"]
(43cm [45.5cm, 51cm, 53.5cm])

14½" [16½", 18¼", 20"]
(37cm [42cm, 46.5cm, 51cm])

Faux Fair Isle Hat

This irresistible baby hat is also irresistibly easy to make! Knit with a self-patterning sock yarn, it looks like a complicated Fair Isle pattern but is really just a one-yarn circular stockinette.

Designer: Lesley Edmondson

Size

Baby: 14″ (35.5cm) head circumference

Toddler: 16″ (40.5cm) head circumference

Child: 18″ (46cm) head circumference

Hat length (all sizes): about 7½″ (19cm) from crown top to unrolled cast-on edge

Note: Finished hat is slightly smaller than the above circumference measurements in order to fit the head snugly.

What You'll Need

Yarn: Wool sock yarn, 164 yards (150m)

We used: Aurora Yarns Strapaz Norweger Ringel (80% superwash wool, 20% nylon; 164 yards [150m] per 50g skein): Color 1 yellow, 1 skein

Needles: US size 4 (3.5mm) circular, 16″ (40cm) long; US size 4 (3.5mm) double-pointed, set of 5

Notions: Open-ring stitch marker; stitch holder; tapestry needle

Gauge

24 stitches and 36 rows=4″ (10cm) in circular stockinette stitch

Notes

• Instructions are given for smallest size; numbers for larger sizes are in brackets. When only 1 number is given, it applies to all sizes.

• Change to double-point needles when there are too few stitches remaining to continue using the circular needles in rounds.

Make the hat

Using size 4 (3.5mm) circular needles, cast on 72 [80, 88] stitches.

Join into a circle, being careful not to twist stitches, and place marker to note beginning of round. Work even in circular stockinette stitch (knit every round) until piece measures 6″ (15cm).

Next round (begin decreases): (Knit 6, knit 2 together) to end of round. (63 [70, 77] stitches)

Round 2 and all even rounds: Knit.

Round 3: (Knit 5, knit 2 together) to end of round. (54 [60, 66] stitches)

Round 5: (Knit 4, knit 2 together) to end of round. (45 [50, 55] stitches)

Round 7: (Knit 3, knit 2 together) to end of round. (36 [40, 44] stitches)
Round 9: (Knit 2, knit 2 together) to end of round. (24 [30, 33] stitches)

Toddler and child sizes only:
Round 11: (Knit 1, knit 2 together) to end of round. ([20, 22] stitches)

All sizes:
Next round: Knit 2 together to end of round. (12 [10, 11] stitches)
Next round: Knit. Remove stitch marker. Do not cut yarn.

Make the I-cord

Divide final 12 [10, 11] stitches as evenly as possible into 2 groups. Slip 1 group of stitches onto stitch holder. Slip remaining stitches onto 1 double-point needle. Using the attached yarn knit 1 row. *Slide the stitches to the other end of needle. The working yarn will be at the "wrong" end of the needle. Strand the yarn across the back of the work and knit 1 row; repeat from * until I-cord measures about 4″ (10cm) in length. *Last row:* Knit 1, knit 2 together, pass slipped stitch over. Cut yarn leaving 4″ (10cm) tail. Pass tail through last stitch on double-point needle to secure. Thread tapestry needle with yarn tail and insert through center of I-cord. Exit I-cord several inches away from where the needle entered. Cut tail and stretch the I-cord slightly so yarn tail disappears into the I-cord center**. Remove remaining stitches from stitch holder and slide onto double-point needle. Join yarn leaving 4″ (10cm) tail and knit 1 row. Repeat I-cord instructions from * to **. Tie both I-cords together with double overhand knot to close hat top. Weave in loose ends securely on wrong side of hat.

Mary Jane Booties

These soft-and-silky booties are as cute as a classic pair of Mary Janes. Knit in the softest cashmere blend, they make a perfect foot covering for baby.

Designer: Lucie Sinkler

Size

0–6 months

Foot length: about 3″ (7.5cm)

Ankle: about 4″ (10cm) circumference with strap buttoned

What You'll Need

Yarn: Sport weight yarn, 137 yards [125m]

We used: Debbie Bliss Baby Cashmerino (55% merino wool, 33% microfiber, 12% cashmere; 137 yards [125 meters] per 50g skein): #605 (blue), #506 (yellow), #601 (pink), 1 skein per pair

Needles: US size 3 (3.25mm)

Notions: Stitch holder; tapestry needle; 2 small buttons, about ¼–½″ (6–1.3cm); sewing needle and thread to match yarn

Gauge

24 stitches and 52 rows=4″ (10cm)

Make the left bootie

Cast on 31 stitches.

Row 1: Knit all stitches.

Row 2: Knit 1, make 1, knit 14, make 1, knit 1, make 1, knit 14, make 1, knit 1. (35 stitches)

Row 3: Knit.

Row 4: Knit 2, make 1, knit 14, make 1, knit 3, make 1, knit 14, make 1, knit 2. (39 stitches)

Row 5: Knit.

Row 6: Knit 3, make 1, knit 14, make 1, knit 5, make 1, knit 14, make 1, knit 3. (43 stitches)

Row 7: Knit.

Row 8: Knit 4, make 1, knit 14, make 1, knit 7, make 1, knit 14, make 1, knit 4. (47 stitches)

Rows 9–17: Knit all stitches.

Row 18: Knit 15, (work slip slip knit decrease) 4 times, knit 1, (knit 2 together) 4 times, knit 15. (39 stitches)

Row 19: Knit.

Row 20: Knit 9, beginning with next 2 stitches bind off 21 stitches, knit across remaining 9 stitches. (This includes 1 stitch already on right needle after the bind-off.)

Put first set of 9 stitches on holder.

Rows 21–23: Knit 9 stitches on needle.

Bind off all 9 stitches; cut yarn.

Rejoin yarn where you started binding off 21 stitches. Cast on 12 stitches using cable cast-on method.

Row 21: Knit across 12 new stitches and 9 from holder. (21 stitches total)

Row 22 (buttonhole row): Knit 18, knit 2 together, yarn over, knit 1. (21 stitches on needle)

Row 23: Knit.

Bind off all stitches.

Make the right bootie

Work same as for left bootie through row 20. Put first set of 9 stitches on holder.

Row 21: Knit 9 stitches on needle; turn work and cast on 12 stitches at end of row using cable cast-on method.
Row 22: Knit 21 stitches (beginning with the 12 new stitches).
Row 23 (buttonhole row): Knit 18, knit 2 together, yarn over, knit 1.
Row 24: Knit all 21 stitches.

Bind off all stitches on needle. Cut yarn leaving 4" (10cm) tail to weave in later. Rejoin yarn to stitches on holder.

Rows 21–23: Knit 9 stitches on needle.

Bind off all stitches.

Finishing

Fold bootie with wrong sides together, and using the invisible seam for garter stitch, sew together back of bootie.

Bottom edges: With wrong sides together, whipstitch cast-on edges together.

Buttons: On the outside of the bootie, opposite the strap side, attach button with sewing needle and matching thread (used doubled), stitching through the holes in the button (or over a button shank) several times. Weave sewing thread through several stitches to secure. (**Note:** Small buttons may pose a choking hazard, so be sure to stitch securely to bootie.)

Weave in all yarn ends to wrong side of work.

Purl of Wisdom

If your buttonholes are not identical, it's best to choose buttons that fit the smallest buttonhole. You can always tighten up the larger buttonholes with scrap yarn and a needle.

Teddy Bear

Your reward for knitting this soft and cuddly teddy bear will be the huge smile on your child's face. What are you waiting for?

Designer: Lucie Sinkler

Size

Length: 12″ (30.5cm) from head to toe

Width: 11″ (28cm) from end of arm to end of arm

What You'll Need

Yarn: Light worsted weight yarn, about 175 yards (160m); black scrap yarn for facial details

We used: Knit One Crochet Too Paint Box (100% wool; 100 yards [91.5m] per 50g skein): #12 Tandoor, 2 skeins

Needles: US size 5 (3.75mm) double-pointed, 2 sets of 4

Notions: Open-ring stitch markers; 4 safety pins; stitch holders; tapestry needle; long sewing pins; fiberfill stuffing

Gauge

20 stitches and 24 rows=4″ (10cm) in stockinette stitch

Make the bear

Leg

Cast on 15 stitches. Divide stitches evenly onto 3 needles and join into circle, taking care not to twist stitches. Place marker.

Round 1: Knit.

Round 2: (Knit 1, make 1) 14 times, knit 1. (29 stitches; 9 stitches on first needle, 10 stitches each on second and third)

Rounds 3–7: Knit.

Round 8: Knit 10, knit 2 together, knit 5, work slip slip knit decrease, knit 10. (27 stitches)

Round 9: Knit 9, knit 2 together, knit 5, work slip slip knit decrease, knit 9. (25 stitches)

Round 10: Knit 8, knit 2 together, knit 5, work slip slip knit decrease, knit 8. (23 stitches)

Round 11: Knit 7, (double-centered decrease: slip 2 stitches as if to knit them together, knit next stitch, pass the slipped stitches over) 3 times, knit 7. (17 stitches)

Rounds 12–16: Knit.

Round 17: Knit 5, make 1, knit 6, make 1, knit 6. (19 stitches)

Rounds 18–21: Knit.

Round 22: Knit 3, make 1, knit 6, make 1, knit 6, make 1, knit 4. (22 stitches)

Rounds 23–26: Knit.

Knit 3, place next 5 stitches on safety pin (inner thigh join). Cut yarn leaving 4″ (10cm) tail to weave in later. Leave the remaining stitches on 3 needles. (17 stitches total)

Second leg

Using the second set of double-point needles, work second leg same as first leg through round 26. Place marker.

Join legs

Continuing with second leg, knit 14 stitches, place next 5 stitches on safety pin. Position the first leg so the safety pins are next to each other where legs meet. Check to make sure both feet are facing the same direction. Do not cut yarn; using the same working yarn, knit across 17 stitches from needles holding the stitches of the first leg, then knit the remaining 3 stitches from second leg to the marker. You will have a circle shape with 34 stitches on needles and 2 safety pins with 5 stitches on each in the middle.

Slip each set of 5 stitches onto a double-point needle. With right sides together, using another (third) needle bind off the 2 sets of 5 stitches together using the 3-needle bind-off method. Cut yarn and secure last stitch.

Body

Round 1: Join yarn, (knit 4, make 1) 4 times, knit 2, (make 1, knit 4) 4 times. (42 stitches)

Rounds 2 and 3: Knit.

Round 4: Knit 1, (knit 10, make 1) 4 times, knit 1. (46 stitches)

Rounds 5–15: Knit.

Round 16: (Knit 9, knit 2 together, knit 10, knit 2 together) 2 times. (42 stitches)

Rounds 17–19: Knit.

Round 20: Knit 4, (knit 2 together, knit 9) 3 times, knit 2 together, knit 3. (38 stitches)

Rounds 21 and 22: Knit.

Leave the 38 body stitches on their needles as temporary stitch holders.

Arm (make 2)

With second set of double-point needles, cast on 6 stitches. Divide stitches evenly onto 3 needles and join into circle, taking care not to twist stitches. Place marker.

Round 1: Knit.

Round 2: (Knit 1, make 1) to end of round. (12 stitches)

Round 3: Knit.

Round 4: (Knit 2, make 1) 6 times. (18 stitches)

Round 5: Knit.

Round 6: (Knit 3, make 1) 6 times. (24 stitches)

Rounds 7–10: Knit.

Round 11: Knit 2, (knit 2 together) 10 times, knit 2. (14 stitches)

Rounds 12–15: Knit.

Round 16: Knit 1, (knit 4, make 1) 3 times, knit 1. (17 stitches)

Rounds 17–19: Knit.
Round 20: Knit 3, (make 1, knit 5) 2 times, make 1, knit 3. (20 stitches)
Rounds 21–23: Knit.
Round 24: Knit 1, (knit 6, make 1) 3 times, knit 1. (23 stitches)
Rounds 25 and 26: Knit.

Place all 23 stitches on holder.

Repeat steps to make second arm.

Join arms to body
Beginning at center back of body, knit across 7 stitches of body; place next 5 stitches of body (underarm) on safety pin. Working with 1 arm at a time, place 5 stitches from the arm on another safety pin for underarm, knit across remaining 18 stitches of arm, knit across 14 stitches of body, place next 5 body stitches on another safety pin for underarm. Working with the second arm, place 5 stitches on safety pin, knit across 18 stitches of second arm. Knit across 7 stitches of body. (64 stitches on needle, and 4 safety pins each with 5 stitches)

Bind off underarm stitches using 3-needle bind-off method.

Next round: Knit 3, *knit 9, knit 2 together; repeat from * 5 times more, knit 4. (58 stitches)

Decrease for shoulders
Round 1: Knit 6, slip next 2 stitches as if to knit them together, knit 1, pass the slipped stitches over the just-worked stitch (double decrease), knit 11, double decrease, knit 12, double decrease, knit 11, double decrease, knit 6. (50 stitches)
Round 2: Knit 5, double decrease, knit 9, double decrease, knit 10, double decrease, knit 9, double decrease, knit 5. (42 stitches)
Round 3: Knit 4, double decrease, knit 7, double decrease, knit 8, double decrease, knit 7, double decrease, knit 4. (34 stitches)
Round 4: Knit 3, double decrease, knit 5, double decrease, knit 6, double decrease, knit 5, double decrease, knit 3. (26 stitches)
Round 5: Knit 2, double decrease, knit 6, double decrease, knit 4, double decrease, knit 6, double decrease, knit 2. (18 stitches)
Rounds 6 and 7: Knit.

Head

Round 1: (Knit 1, make 1) 17 times, knit 1. (35 stitches)

Rounds 2 and 3: Knit.

Round 3: (Knit 4, make 1) 8 times. (43 stitches)

Rounds 4–7: Knit.

Round 8: Knit 21, make 1, knit 22. (44 stitches)

Round 9: Knit.

Round 10: Knit 20, make 1, knit 3, make 1, knit 21. (46 stitches)

Rounds 11 and 12: Knit.

Round 13: Knit 19, knit 2 together, knit 4, work slip slip knit decrease, knit 19. (44 stitches)

Round 14: Knit.

Round 15: Knit 18, knit 2 together, double decrease, work slip slip knit decrease, knit 19. (40 stitches)

Rounds 16–19: Knit.

Round 20: Knit 3, knit 2 together, knit 4, double decrease, (knit 3, knit 2 together) 2 times, knit 4, double decrease, knit 3, knit 2 together, knit 3. (32 stitches)

Round 21: Knit 2, knit 2 together, knit 4, double decrease, (knit 2, knit 2 together) 2 times, knit 4, double decrease, knit 2, knit 2 together, knit 2. (24 stitches)

Round 22: (Knit 2 together) 12 times. (12 stitches)

Cut yarn leaving 6″ (15cm) tail. Thread tail on tapestry needle, pull through remaining stitches, and fasten off.

Ear (make 2)

Cast on 3 stitches.

Row 1: Knit into front and back of first and second stitch, knit 1. (5 stitches)

Row 2 (and all even rows): Purl.

Row 3: Knit into front and back of first stitch, knit 2, knit into front and back of next stitch, knit 1. (7 stitches)

Row 5: Knit.

Row 7: Work slip slip knit decrease, knit 3, knit 2 together. (5 stitches)

Row 9: Work slip slip knit decrease, knit 1, knit 2 together. (3 stitches)

Row 11: Knit 3 together.

Cut yarn and fasten off.

Repeat steps to make second ear.

Fold ears in half. Pin in place at top of head, matching loose edges. With yarn threaded on tapestry needle, whipstitch ears in place.

Stuff bear with fiberfill as evenly as possible, filling through opening in feet. Whipstitch feet closed. Using black yarn threaded on tapestry needle, complete facial features by embroidering an "X" for each eye, a diamond shape for the nose, and 2 lines for the mouth.

Penguin Pal Hat

This cheerful cap is as cool as can be, but it's sure to keep any child warm.
Once you get the hang of knitting from a chart, you may play around with
more designs to see which other animals would make a cute hat!

Designer: Lucie Sinkler

Size

Circumference: 16" (40.5cm)
Height: 7" (18cm)

What You'll Need

Yarn: Worsted weight wool yarn,
approximately 95 yards (87m) color A;
30 yards (27.5m) color B; about 15 yards
(14m) color C

We used: Cascade 220 (100% wool;
220 yards [201m] per 3½oz [100g] skein):
#8555 black (color A), 1 skein;
#7824 orange (color B), 1 skein;
#8505 white (color C), 1 skein

Needles: US size 6 (4mm)

Notion: Tapestry needle

Gauge

20 stitches and 32 rows=4" (10cm)
in stockinette stitch

Note: When changing colors, drop the old
color and bring the new color up from under
the old color, twisting them together to avoid
gaps (see Changing Colors, page 21). For
each section being worked, you will need
2 balls color A, 1 ball color B, and 2 small
balls color C.

Make the hat

With color B cast on 80 stitches. Work
8 rows in stockinette stitch (knit 1 row,
purl 1 row).

Work 4 rows in (knit 1, purl 1) ribbing.
Cut color B.

Next row (right side): With first ball of
color A knit 30, drop A; join color C, knit
20, drop color C; join second ball of A,
knit 30, turn work.

Row 2: Still working with second ball of
A, purl 30, drop A; pick up color C, purl
20, drop C; pick up first ball of A, purl 30,
turn work.

Repeat these 2 rows seven times more.

Start row 1 (right-side row) of chart.
Follow chart for next 14 rows using
separate balls of yarn for each area.

Decrease rows

Row 1 (right side): With yarn A, (knit 8,
knit 2 together) 8 times. (72 stitches)

Rows 2, 4, and 6: Purl.

Row 8: (Purl 2 together, purl 4) 8 times. (40 stitches)

Row 9: (Knit 3, knit 2 together) 8 times. (32 stitches)

Row 10: (Purl 2 together, purl 2) 8 times. (24 stitches)

Row 11: (Knit 2 together, knit 1) 8 times. (16 stitches)

Row 12: (Purl 2 together) to end of row. (8 stitches)

Cut yarn leaving about 20″ (51cm) tail. Thread tail through tapestry needle and slip needle through remaining 8 live stitches. Pull yarn tail gently to draw stitches together snugly, and fasten off. Sew back seam using mattress stitch. Weave in all loose ends to inside of hat.

Row 3: (Knit 7, knit 2 together) 8 times. (64 stitches)

Row 5: (Knit 6, knit 2 together) 8 times. (56 stitches)

Row 7: (Knit 5, knit 2 together) 8 times. (48 stitches)

Key
- ▦ Black
- ☐ White
- ▦ Orange

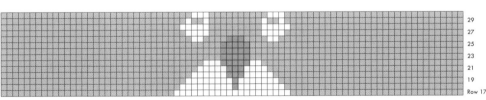

Pretty Poncho

This multicolor poncho is worked in one piece, starting at the bottom edge. Fringe is added at the end to make it even more fabulous. It's a little girl's dream!

Designer: Lucie Sinkler

Size

Fits 18–24 months

Length (including fringe): 16″ (40.5cm)

What You'll Need

Yarn: Bulky weight multicolor yarn, about 286 yards (262m) yarn A; worsted weight solid-color yarn, about 200 yards (183m) yarn B

We used: Plymouth Encore Colorspin chunky (75% acrylic, 25% wool; 143 yards [131m] per 100g skein): #7124 (yarn A), 2 skeins; Plymouth Encore worsted (75% acrylic, 25% wool; 200 yards [183m] per 100g skein): #1382 (yarn B), 1 skein

Needles: US size 10 (6mm) circular, 24″ (61cm) long

Notions: Open-ring stitch markers (2 colors); tapestry needle; size H/8 (5mm) crochet hook

Gauge

14 stitches and 21 rounds=4″ (10cm) in circular stockinette stitch (knit all rounds)

Make the poncho

With yarn A, cast on 180 stitches. Place marker and join in round, taking care not to twist stitches.

Bottom edging

Round 1: Purl.

Round 2: (Knit 2 stitches together, yarn over) to end of round.

Round 3: Purl.

Round 4: Knit.

Establish places for decreases

Remove end-of-round marker.

Round 5 (right side): Knit 1, work slip slip knit decrease, knit 84, knit 2 together, place marker, knit 2, work slip slip knit decrease, knit 84, knit 2 together, place marker, knit 1. (176 stitches)

Rounds 6 and 7: Knit, slipping markers from left to right needle as you meet them.

Round 8: Knit 1, work slip slip knit decrease, knit 82, knit 2 together, slip marker, knit 2, work slip slip knit decrease, knit 82, knit 2 together, slip 2 together, knit 1. (172 stitches)

Repeat rounds 6–8 decreasing 4 stitches every third round in established places until there is a total of 124 stitches and piece measures about 9″ (23cm) from cast-on edge.

Split for the neck opening

Begin working back and forth in rows as follows:

Row 1 (right side): Knit 1, work slip slip knit decrease, knit to 2 stitches before next marker, knit 2 together, slip marker, knit 2, work slip slip knit decrease, knit to 2 stitches before next marker, knit 2 together, knit 1. Turn work. (120 stitches)

Row 2: Purl.

Repeat rows 1 and 2 until 92 stitches remain and neck opening is about 3″ (7.5cm) long. End with row 1.

Shape shoulders

Before turning work to begin row 2, place a stitch marker after stitch 23 (counting stitches from beginning of row) and another marker after stitch 69.

Note: To mark decreases for shoulder shaping, use a different color stitch marker than previously used.

Row 2: Purl, slipping all markers in place.
Next row (right side): Knit 1, work slip slip knit decrease, knit to 2 stitches before new marker, decrease 2 stitches using the vertical double decrease method as follows: Slip 2 stitches as if to knit them together, remove marker, knit 1, pass the 2 slipped stitches over the knit stitch, place marker, knit to 2 stitches before marker in the center of back, knit 2 together, knit 2, work slip slip knit decrease, knit to 2 stitches before second shoulder marker, decrease 2 stitches same as first shoulder, place marker, knit to 2 stitches before next marker, knit 2 together, knit 1. (84 stitches)

Next row: Purl.

Repeat these last 2 rows until 52 stitches remain, ending with knit (right-side) row.

Neck edging

Row 1 (wrong side): Knit.
Row 2: Knit 1, (knit 2 together, yarn over) to last 3 stitches, knit 2 together, knit 1.
Row 3: Knit.

Bind off loosely. Weave in loose ends to wrong side of work.

Finishing

Make the fringe

For each fringe, cut one 10″ (25.5cm) strand yarn A and two 10″ (25.5cm) strands yarn B. (90 bunches, or 270 strands, total)

Place poncho flat on table. Insert the crochet hook from back to front into a hole in the bottom edging. Working with 1 strand yarn A and 2 strands yarn B at a time, fold them in half and hold cut ends together to create a loop. Place folded loop on hook and pull it halfway through the knitted piece. With hook still in place, pull cut ends of fringe through the loop to make knot. Pull fringe ends to tighten. Repeat making fringe around poncho.

Make the I-cord

With yarn B cast on 3 stitches and knit I-cord about 28″ (71cm) long (see page 22). Thread I-cord through the holes in the neck edging.

Make the tassels

Wrap yarn A around 5 fingers about 10 times, cut yarn. Cut a 6″ (15cm) strand of yarn A, thread through the wrapped yarn, and tie both ends of the 6″ (15cm) strand into a double knot. Thread both ends onto tapestry needle and stitch securely to end of I-cord; weave ends into center of I-cord to hide. Cut another 6″ (15cm) strand of yarn A and wrap around yarn bunch about ½″ (1.3cm) down from tassel top. Tie both ends of this strand into a double knot and allow remaining 2 ends to hang with the tassel strands. Cut through bottom loops of yarn bunch; trim ends to even length. Repeat for second tassel.

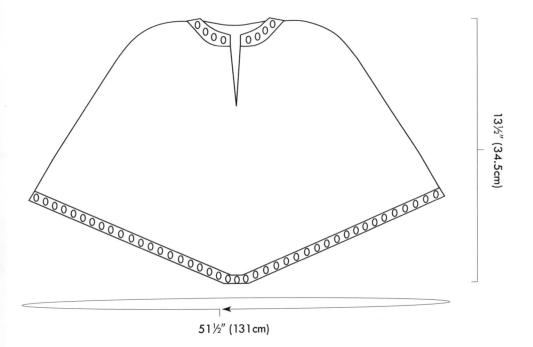

13½″ (34.5cm)

51½″ (131cm)

Plush Pullover

The sweater is made with soft, plush yarn that is lighter than air yet cozy and warm. The pattern is quick and easy to make. Buttoned openings at both sides of the neck make dressing baby easy.

Designer: Kathy Perry

Size

6 months: 21″ (53.5cm) chest
12 months: 22″ (56cm) chest
18 months: 23″ (58.5cm) chest

What You'll Need

Yarn: Soft, synthetic bulky weight yarn, about 270 yards (247m)

We used: Berroco Plush Colors (100% nylon; 90 yards [83m] per 50g ball): #1952 Baby Mix, 3 balls; #1924 Jazzy Turquoise, 1–2 yards (.92–1.83m) for blanket stitch trim

Needles: US size 8 (5mm)

Notions: Tapestry needle; 4 stitch markers; safety pins; needle and thread to match yarn; 6 novelty buttons (about ½″ [.33cm] diameter)

Gauge

15 stitches and 22 rows=4″ (10cm) in stockinette stitch

Note: Instructions are given for smallest size; numbers for larger sizes are in brackets. When only 1 number is given, it applies to all sizes.

Make the sweater

Back

Cast on 40 [42, 44] stitches. Work in stockinette stitch (knit on right side, purl on wrong side) until piece measures 5½″ [7″, 7″] (14cm [18cm, 18cm]) in length from cast-on edge, and place marker at both ends for beginning of armholes.

Continue in stockinette stitch until piece measures 9½″ [12″, 12½″] (24cm [30.5cm, 31.5cm]) from cast-on edge. Bind off all stitches.

Front

Work as for back until last 3 rows, ending with a purl row.

Buttonhole row: Knit 2, knit 2 together, yarn over, knit 1, knit 2 together, yarn over, knit 1, knit 2 together, yarn over, knit 20 [22, 24], knit 2 together, yarn over, knit 1, knit 2 together, yarn over, knit 1, knit 2 together, yarn over, knit 2.

Next row: Purl, working the yarnovers as stitches.

Next row: Knit.

Bind off in purl stitches.

Sleeves (make 2)

Cast on 23 [24, 25] stitches. Work in stockinette stitch, increasing 1 stitch at each end of work every 6 rows 4 [0, 0] times, then 1 stitch each end every 0 [5, 5] rows 0 [7, 8] times. (31 [38, 41] stitches on needle)

Work even until sleeve measures 6" [7", 7½"] (15cm [18cm, 19cm]). Bind off.

Repeat steps for second sleeve.

Finishing

With right sides up, overlap front and back pieces by 1" (1.3cm) at neck edges with front piece on top. Pin in place. Pin sleeves to body of sweater, easing to fit between markers. With yarn threaded on tapestry needle, sew sleeves to body using the backstitch seam. Sew side and sleeve seams using mattress stitch. Mark placement of buttons on back shoulders of sweater under the front overlap to align with buttonholes; sew buttons securely in place. *Note:* Small buttons may pose a choking hazard, so be sure to attach them securely and check each time after washing.

Make a blanket stitch or overcast stitch edging with contrasting-color yarn around the lower edges of sleeves and sweater.

Weave in all yarn ends to wrong side of work.

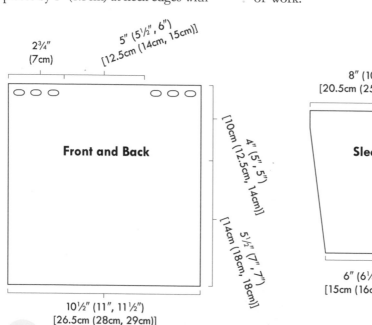

2¾"
(7cm)

5" (5½", 6")
[12.5cm (14cm, 15cm)]

Front and Back

4" (5", 5")
[10cm (12.5cm, 14cm)]

5½" (7", 7")
[14cm (18cm, 18cm)]

10½" (11", 11½")
[26.5cm (28cm, 29cm)]

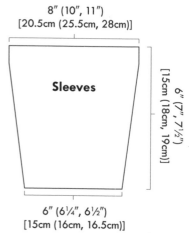

8" (10", 11")
[20.5cm (25.5cm, 28cm)]

Sleeves

6" (7", 7½")
[15cm (18cm, 19cm)]

6" (6¼", 6½")
[15cm (16cm, 16.5cm)]

Houndstooth Blanket

Worked in crisp, contrasting colors, this blanket is sophisticated as well as cozy and warm. Its simple-to-knit slip-stitch pattern uses only one color yarn per row so you don't have to carry two colors.

Designer: Susan Leitzsch

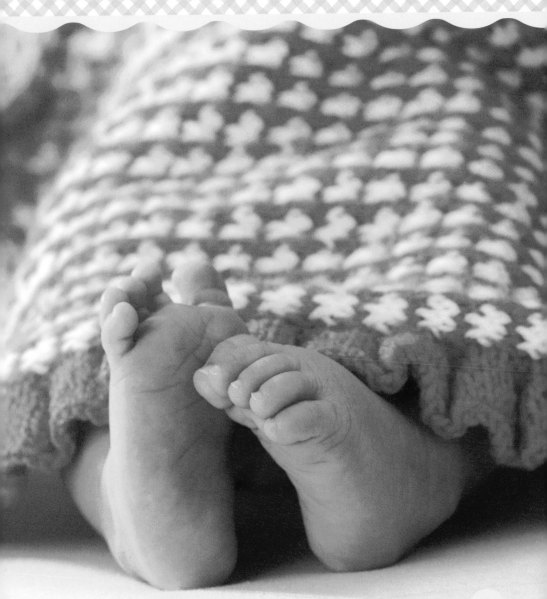

Size

Approximately 42×40″ (106.5×101.5cm), including ruffle edge

What You'll Need

Yarn: Soft sport weight yarn, 918 yards (839.5m) each in 2 colors

We used: Lion Brand Babysoft (60% acrylic, 40% nylon; 459 yards [420m] per 5oz ball): #100 White (color A), 2 skeins; #184 Melon (color B), 2 skeins

Needles: US size 7 (4.5mm)

Notion: Tapestry needle

Gauge

22 stitches and 31 rows=4″ (10cm) in pattern

Notes

• Carry unused yarn loosely along edge; do not cut yarn at end of each color.

• When slipping stitches, slip as if to purl.

Make the blanket

With color B, cast on 216 stitches very loosely.

Row 1 (right side): Drop color B. Join color A and knit 1, *with yarn in back slip 1 as if to purl, knit 2; repeat from * to last 2 stitches, with yarn in back slip 1 as if to purl, knit 1.

Row 2: With color A, purl.

Row 3: Drop color A, pick up color B, *with yarn in back slip 1 as if to purl, knit 2; repeat from * across row.

Row 4: With color B, purl.

Repeat rows 1–4 until piece measures about 36½″ (92.5cm) ending with row 4.

Make the border

Side edge

Using color B, with right side facing pick up and knit 270 stitches evenly spaced across 1 side edge.

Row 1: (Knit 3, purl 2) across row.

Row 2: (Knit 1, knit in front and back of next stitch, purl 3) across row. (324 stitches)

Row 3: (Knit 3, purl 2, purl in front and back of next stitch) across row. (378 stitches)

Row 4: (Knit 3, knit in front and back of next stitch, purl 3) across row. (432 stitches)

Row 5: (Knit 3, purl 4, make 1 purlwise, purl 1) across row. (486 stitches)
Row 6: (Knit 6, purl 3) across row.
Row 7: (Knit 3, purl 6) across row.

Bind off loosely in pattern. Repeat for other side edge.

Bottom edge: Using color B, with right side facing pick up and knit 215 stitches evenly spaced across cast-on edge.

Work rows 1–7 same as for side edge. (***Note:*** Increase rows will have fewer stitches than side edge. You'll increase 43 stitches on each increase row.) Bind off all stitches loosely in pattern.

Repeat for upper edge across the bind-off edge.

Weave in all yarn ends to wrong side of work.

Purl of Wisdom

Make 1 purlwise: Insert left needle from back to front under the horizontal strand between the last stitch on the right needle and the first stitch on the left needle, then purl through the front loop.

Daisy-top Hat

You've never had this much fun playing up-see-daisy! This fantastic hat is highlighted with whimsical daisy petals and easy-to-work embroidered flowers.

Designer: Cathleen Stephen

Size

Small: 14″ (35.5cm) circumference at lower edge

Large: 16″ (40.5cm) circumference at lower edge

What You'll Need

Yarn: 100% wool sport weight yarn, about 100 [125] yards (91.5 [114]m) color A; 100 [125] yards (91.5 [114]m) color B; 50 yards (46m) color C; 5 yards (4.5m) color D

We used: Brown Sheep Company Nature Spun Sport (100% wool; 184 yards [168m] per 50g skein): #N109 Spring Green (color A), #N78 Turquoise Wonder (color B), #730 Natural (color C), 1 skein each color; #305 Imperial Yellow (color D) **Note:** Only a small amount of color D is needed to make the daisy center (about 5 yards [4.5m]). Any scrap yellow sport weight yarn will work.

Needles: US size 10½ (6.5mm) double-pointed, set of 4 or 5; US size 7 (4.5mm)

Notions: Open-ring stitch marker; tapestry needle

Gauge

14 stitches and 19 rows=4″ (10cm) in stockinette stitch

Notes

• Instructions are given for small size; numbers for larger size are in brackets. When only 1 number is given, it applies to both sizes.

• Hat is worked with 2 strands held together as 1. Use single strand of yarn to make daisy and embroidery.

Make the hat

With 2 strands of color A held together as 1 and size 10½ (6.5mm) double-point needles, cast on 50 [55] stitches. Divide stitches equally as possible on 3 or 4 double-point needles and join work into circle, taking care not to twist stitches. Place marker at beginning of round. Work in circular stockinette stitch (knit every round) for 16 [18] rounds.

Cut yarn A leaving 4″ (10cm) tails; join B (holding 2 strands together as 1) and continue in stockinette stitch for 6 [8] more rounds.

Shape the top

Round 1 (right side): *Knit 8 [9], knit 2 together; repeat from * to end of round. (45 [50] stitches)

Rounds 2, 4, 6, 8, 10, and 12: Knit, without making decreases.

Round 3: *Knit 7 [8], knit 2 together; repeat from * to end of round. (40 [45] stitches)

Round 5: *Knit 6 [7], knit 2 together; repeat from * to end of round. (35 [40] stitches)

Round 7: *Knit 5 [6], knit 2 together; repeat from * to end of round. (30 [35] stitches)

Round 9: *Knit 4 [5], knit 2 together; repeat from * to end of round. (25 [30] stitches)

Round 11: *Knit 3 [4], knit 2 together; repeat from * to end of round. (20 [25] stitches)

Round 13: Knit 2 together to end of round [end larger size with knit 1]. (10 [13] stitches)

Round 14: Knit 2 together to end of round [end larger size with knit 1]. (5 [7] stitches)

Cut yarn leaving 6″ (15cm) tail. Thread tail onto tapestry needle and pull through remaining stitches. Gently pull on yarn tail to draw stitches together and close top of hat. Weave in tail to inside of hat.

Embroider flowers

With tapestry needle and single strand of color A, embroider 5 stem/leaf combinations evenly spaced around the hat with stem bottoms aligned where colors A and B meet. With color C, embroider daisy petals above stems as shown in photo.

Make flower petals (make 5)

With size 7 (4.5mm) needles and single strand of color C, cast on 3 stitches. Work in rows as follows:

Row 1 (wrong side): Purl.

Row 2 (right side): Slip 1 stitch knitwise, increase 1 stitch using the make 1 (right-leaning) method, knit to last stitch, increase 1 stitch using the make 1 (left-leaning) method, knit 1. (5 stitches on needle)

Row 3: Slip 1 purlwise, purl to end of row.

Repeat rows 2 and 3 until there are 9 stitches on needle. Work even for 6 more rows, ending with wrong-side row.

Decrease for petal point:

Row 1 (right side): Slip 2 stitches knit-wise, 1 at a time to right needle, insert left needle tip through fronts of both stitches from left to right, knit them together in this position (slip slip knit decrease), knit to last 2 stitches, knit these 2 stitches together. (7 stitches)

Row 2: Purl.

Repeat rows 1 and 2 until 3 stitches remain, ending with right-side row.

Next row (wrong side): Slip 1 stitch purlwise, purl 2 together, pass slipped stitch over last stitch and fasten off.

Weave in loose ends and lightly press. With color C threaded on tapestry needle, using whipstitch sew petal points to top center of hat so the 5 points are touching each other.

Daisy center: With size 7 (4.5mm) needles and color D, loosely cast on 1 stitch leaving 6″ (15cm) tail.

Row 1 (right side): Knit into front and back of this stitch 3 times (6 stitches).
Rows 2 and 4: Purl.
Rows 3 and 5: Knit.
Row 6: (Purl 2 together) across row. (3 stitches)
Row 7: Slip 1 stitch knitwise, knit 2 together, pass slipped stitch over last stitch.

Cut yarn leaving 6″ (15cm) tail. Tie both tails (beginning and end) together, thread through tapestry needle and pull through top of hat so bobble is in center of petals. Secure tail to inside of hat.

Felted Block Set

Knit up this delightful set of soft felted baby blocks in bright primary colors. The three different sizes are perfect for tossing, stacking, and knocking down.

Designer: Chrissy Gardiner

Size

Small block:

Approximately 3½×5" (9×12.5cm) before felting

Approximately 3×3" (7.5×7.5cm) after felting

Medium block:

Approximately 5×6½" (12.5×16.5cm) before felting

Approximately 4×4" (10×10cm) after felting

Large block:

Approximately 6×8" (15×20.5cm) before felting

Approximately 5×5" (12.5×12.5cm) after felting

What You'll Need

Yarn: 100% wool worsted weight yarn, about 93 yards (85m) for small block, 152 yards (139m) for medium block, 247 yards (226m) for large block

We used: Knit Picks Wool of the Andes (100% wool; 110 yards [101m] per 50g ball): small block #23440 Blue Bonnet, 1 ball; medium block #23436 Daffodil, 2 balls; large block #23431 Tomato, 3 balls

Needles: US size 8 (5mm)

Notions: Tapestry needle; sewing needle and thread to match yarn color(s); fiberfill stuffing

Gauge

18 stitches and 24 rows=4" (10cm) in stockinette stitch before felting

Notes

• Instructions are given for smallest size; numbers for larger sizes are in brackets. When only 1 number is given, it applies to all sizes.

• Each block is knitted and felted in 6 pieces, then sewn together with sewing needle and matching thread.

Make the blocks

Cast on 17 [22, 27] stitches.

Rows 1–5: Knit.

Row 6 (wrong side): Knit 3, purl 11 [16, 21], knit 3.

Row 7: Knit.

Repeat rows 6 and 7 nine [14, 19] times more.

Knit 2 more rows. Bind off loosely. Weave in yarn ends to wrong side of work.

Repeat to make 6 pieces for each block size.

Felting

Felt pieces in washing machine (see Felting, page 32).

Finishing

With sewing needle and thread whipstitch 5 of the 6 pieces of each block together into the start of a cube shape. Sew 3 of the 4 edges of the last piece to the cube, then stuff block with fiberfill stuffing. Sew last edge of block. If needed, gently brush edges with a toothbrush to hide stitches.

Cabled Cardigan

This cardigan makes a wonderful lightweight jacket or warm sweater for baby. Machine washable and oh-so-soft, the yarn comes in a wonderful array of colors and is shown off to best advantage in a delicate cable pattern.

Designer: Beth Walker-O'Brien

Size

0–6 months: chest 19" (48.5cm), length 9" (23cm)

6–12 months: chest 22" (56cm), length 10" (25.5cm)

2 years: chest 25" (63.5cm), length 12½" (31.5cm)

3 years: chest 28" (71cm), length 13½" (34.5cm)

What You'll Need

Yarn: Worsted weight yarn, about 504 [504, 588, 672] yards (462m [462m, 538m, 614.5m])

We used: Lion Brand Yarns Cashmere Blend (72% merino wool, 14% cashmere, 14% nylon; 84 yards [77m] per 40g skein): #105 Light Blue, 6 [6, 7, 8] balls

Needles: US size 8 (5mm); US size 8 (5mm) double-pointed, set of 2 (for closing hood seam)

Notions: 3 stitch holders; tapestry needle; 10" (25.5cm) long separating zipper in color to match yarn; long sewing pins; sewing needle and thread in color to match yarn

Gauge

21 stitches and 24 rows=4" (10cm) in Baby Cable Ribbing Stitch

Notes

• Instructions are given for smallest size; numbers for larger sizes are in brackets. When only 1 number is given, it applies to all sizes.

• A "cable 2 twist" is worked as follows: Knit 2 together leaving stitches on left needle, insert right needle between 2 stitches just knitted together and knit the first stitch again, slip both stitches from left needle.

• Follow the Baby Cable Ribbing Stitch pattern instructions written specifically for the left front, right front, and hood pieces as they include slip stitch selvage instructions that are not included in the Baby Cable Ribbing Stitch pattern given below.

Baby Cable Ribbing Stitch

Rows 1 and 3 (wrong side): Knit 2, *purl 2, knit 2; repeat from * to end of row.

Row 2: Purl 2, *cable 2 twist (see "Notes"), purl 2; repeat from * to end of row.

Row 4: Purl 2, *knit 2, purl 2; repeat from * to end of row.

Make the cardigan
Back

Cast on 50 [58, 66, 74] stitches.

Work the Baby Cable Ribbing Stitch pattern starting with row 1. Continue in

pattern until piece measures 9" [10", 12½", 13½"] (23cm [25.5cm, 32cm, 34cm]) or desired length. Place stitches on holder.

Left front

Cast on 26 [30, 34, 38] stitches.

Row 1 (wrong side): Knit 2, *purl 2, knit 2; repeat from * to end.

Row 2: Slip 1 purlwise with yarn in front, purl 1, *cable 2 twist, purl 2; repeat from * to end of row.

Row 3: Knit 2, *purl 2, knit 2; repeat from * to end of row.

Row 4: Slip 1 purlwise with yarn in front, purl 1, *knit 2, purl 2; repeat from * to end of row.

Continue in established pattern until piece measures about 8" [9", 11", 11½"] (20.5cm [23cm, 28cm, 29cm]) or desired length, ending with a wrong-side row.

Keeping in pattern, work neck shaping as follows:

Next right-side row: Bind off 4 stitches at neck edge 1 time, work remaining stitches in pattern. (22 [26, 30, 34] stitches)

All wrong-side rows: Work in established pattern, adjusting as necessary to accommodate changing stitch count.

Next right-side row: Bind off 3 stitches at neck edge, work remaining stitches in pattern. (19 [23, 27, 31] stitches)

Next right-side row *(2 smallest sizes only):* Bind off 2 stitches at neck edge, work remaining stitches in pattern. (17 [21] stitches)

Next 2 right-side rows *(2 largest sizes only):* Bind off 2 stitches at neck edge on this row and the next *right-side* row, work remaining stitches in pattern. (23 [27] stitches)

Next right-side row *(all sizes):* Knit 2 together at neck edge, work remaining stitches in pattern. (16 [20, 22, 26] stitches)

Next right-side row *(largest size only):* Knit 2 together at neck edge, work remaining stitches in pattern. (25 stitches)

Work even in pattern until piece measures about 9" [10", 12½", 13½"] (23cm [25.5cm, 32cm, 34cm]). Place 16 [20, 22, 25] shoulder stitches on holder.

Right front

Cast on 26 [30, 34, 38] stitches.

Rows 1 and 3 (wrong side): Slip 1 purl-wise with yarn in front, knit 1, *purl 2, knit 2; repeat from * to end.

Row 2: *Purl 2, cable 2 twist; repeat from * until 2 stitches remain, purl 1, knit 1.

Row 4: *Purl 2, knit 2; repeat from * until 2 stitches remain, purl 1, knit 1.

Continue in pattern until piece measures 8″ [9″, 11″, 11½″] (20.5cm [23cm, 28cm, 29cm]) or desired length, ending with a wrong-side row.

Next right-side row: Bind off 4 stitches at neck edge 1 time, work remaining stitches in pattern. (22 [26, 30, 34] stitches)

All wrong-side rows: Work in established pattern, adjusting as necessary to accommodate changing stitch count.

Next right-side row: Bind off 3 stitches at neck edge, work remaining stitches in pattern. (19 [23, 27, 31] stitches)

Next right-side row (2 smallest sizes only): Bind off 2 stitches at neck edge, work remaining stitches in pattern. (17 [21] stitches)

Next 2 right-side rows (2 largest sizes only): Bind off 2 stitches at neck edge on this row and the next *right-side* row, work remaining stitches in pattern. (23 [27] stitches)

Next right-side row (all sizes): Work slip slip knit decrease at neck edge, work remaining stitches in pattern. (16 [20, 22, 26] stitches)

Next right-side row (largest size only): Work slip slip knit decrease at neck edge, work remaining stitches in pattern. (25 stitches)

Work even in pattern until piece measures 9″ [10″, 12½″, 13½″] (23cm [25.5cm, 32cm, 34cm]). Place 16 [20, 22, 25] shoulder stitches on holder.

Sleeves (make 2)

Cast on 26 [30, 34, 38] stitches.

Work the Baby Cable Ribbing Stitch pattern while *at the same time* using the make 1 increase method to increase 1 stitch at each sleeve edge every fourth row 10 [11, 12, 13] times. (50 [52, 58, 64] stitches)

Continue in pattern until sleeve length measures 6¾″ [7½″, 8¾″, 9″] (17cm [19cm, 22cm, 23cm]). Bind off.

Repeat for second sleeve.

Working from armhole toward neck, seam shoulder stitches of left front to shoulder stitches of back using 3-needle bind-off technique. Repeat seaming for right shoulder. Leave remaining 20 [20, 24, 26] back neck stitches on holder for neck (the stitch count includes the remaining stitch on each shoulder after completing the bind-off).

Hood

Beginning at right center front neck opening (as worn) with right side facing, pick up 42 [42, 46, 50] stitches around neck edge toward the left center front (as worn).

Row 1 (wrong side): Slip 1 purlwise with yarn in front, knit 1, (purl 2, knit 1 into front and back of next stitch) 4 times, (purl 2, knit 2) 3 [3, 4, 5] times, (purl 2, knit 1 into front and back of next stitch) 4 times, purl 2, knit 2. (50 [50, 54, 58] stitches)

Row 2: Slip 1 purlwise with yarn in front, purl 1, *cable 2 twist, purl 2; repeat from * until 4 stitches remain, cable 2 twist, purl 1, knit 1.

Row 3: Slip 1 purlwise with yarn in front, knit 1, *purl 2, knit 2; repeat from * to end of row.

Row 4: Slip 1 purlwise with yarn in front, purl 1, *knit 2, purl 2; repeat from * until 4 stitches remain, knit 2, purl 1, knit 1.

Row 5: Slip 1 purlwise with yarn in front, knit 1, *purl 2, knit 2; repeat from * to end of row.

Repeat rows 2–5 until hood measures 7½" [8", 8½", 9"] (19cm [20.5cm, 21.5cm, 23cm]) in length.

Divide hood stitches in half, placing 25 [25, 27, 29] stitches each onto their own double-point needle. Holding double-point needles parallel to each other with wrong sides of fabric facing (right sides together), join the stitches from both needles using the 3-needle bind-off technique to close the hood top.

Finishing

Center top of sleeves on shoulder seams and with yarn threaded on tapestry needle use mattress stitch to attach sleeves to body. Sew side and sleeve seams with mattress stitch. Pin zipper in position, aligning bottom of zipper with bottom edge of knitted pieces and placing vertical edges of center front knitted pieces next to the teeth. If the zipper extends past the top edge, separate the zipper and trim the top of each side to match the exact length. Using matching color sewing thread and sewing needle, stitch a dozen or so times around an individual tooth just below the trimmed edge to create a stop for the zipper pull. Using sewing thread and sewing needle and with right side facing, backstitch zipper in place along the vertical edge of the knitted fronts. Whipstitch edges of zipper tape in place with wrong side facing. Remove all pins. Weave in all loose ends to wrong side of sweater.

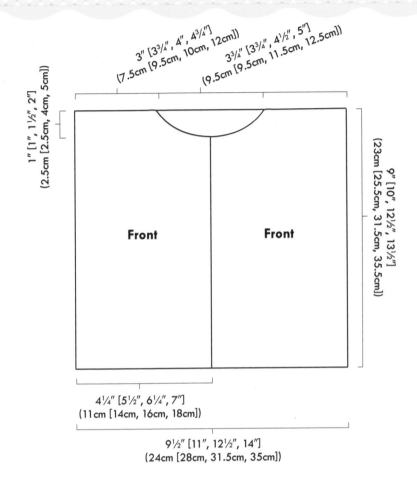

3" [3¾", 4", 4¾"]
(7.5cm [9.5cm, 10cm, 12cm])

3¾" [3¾", 4½", 5"]
(9.5cm [9.5cm, 11.5cm, 12.5cm])

1" [1", 1½", 2"]
(2.5cm [2.5cm, 4cm, 5cm])

9" [10", 12½", 13½"]
(23cm [25.5cm, 31.5cm, 35.5cm])

Front

Front

4¼" [5½", 6¼", 7"]
(11cm [14cm, 16cm, 18cm])

9½" [11", 12½", 14"]
(24cm [28cm, 31.5cm, 35cm])

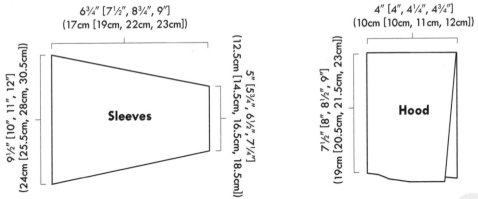

6¾" [7½", 8¾", 9"]
(17cm [19cm, 22cm, 23cm])

9½" [10", 11", 12"]
(24cm [25.5cm, 28cm, 30.5cm])

5" [5¾", 6½", 7¼"]
(12.5cm [14.5cm, 16.5cm, 18.5cm])

Sleeves

4" [4", 4¼", 4¾"]
(10cm [10cm, 11cm, 12cm])

7½" [8", 8½", 9"]
(19cm [20.5cm, 21.5cm, 23cm])

Hood

Hooded Towel

Made with soft and absorbent cotton yarn, this hooded bath towel is not only useful, but also unique. Three vertical panels are sewn together to form one large square, and a separate triangular piece is added in one corner to form a hood.

Designer: Kathy Perry

Size

Approximately 30×30″ (76×76cm), including crochet edge

What You'll Need

Yarn: Cotton worsted weight yarn, approximately 472 yards (424m) color A, 236 yards (212m) color B, and about 200 yards (183m) color C

We used: Lion Brand Lion Cotton (100% cotton; 236 yards [212m] per 5oz [142g] ball): #148 Turquoise (color A), 2 balls; #147 Purple (color B), 1 ball; #123 Seaspray (color C), 1 ball

Needles: US size 7 (4.5mm)

Notions: Tapestry needle; long sewing pins; size 8/H (5mm) crochet hook

Gauge

16¾ stitches and 22 rows=4″ (10cm) in stockinette stitch

Note: When joining and ending each color leave a 4″ (10cm) tail to weave in later.

Make the towel

Panel 1

With color A, cast on 40 stitches.
Row 1 (right side): Knit.
Row 2: Purl.

Work even in stockinette stitch (knit on right side, purl on wrong side) until piece measures 9½″ (24cm). Cut yarn. Join color B, continue in stockinette stitch for an additional 9½″ (24cm). Cut yarn. Join color A, continue in stockinette stitch for an additional 9½″ (24cm), ending with wrong-side row. Bind off loosely. Weave in loose ends.

Panel 2

With color B, cast on 40 stitches.
Row 1 (right side): Knit.
Row 2: Purl.

Work even in stockinette stitch until piece measures 9½″ (24cm). Cut yarn. Join color A, continue in stockinette stitch for an additional 9½″ (24cm). Cut yarn. Join color B, continue in stockinette stitch for an additional 9½″ (24cm), ending with wrong-side row. Bind off loosely. Weave in loose ends.

Panel 3

Work as for panel 1.

Make the hood

Using color A, cast on 54 stitches.
Rows 1–3: Knit.
Row 4 (wrong side): Purl.
Row 5 (right side): Work slip slip knit decrease using first 2 stitches, knit to last 2 stitches, knit 2 together. (52 stitches)

Row 6: Purl.

Continue in stockinette stitch, repeating row 5 every other row (right-side rows only,) for a total of 17 times. (18 stitches remain) **Next 8 rows:** Work decreases every row until 4 stitches remain, working as follows: **Right-side rows:** Repeat row 5. **Wrong-side rows:** Purl 2 together, purl to last 2 stitches, work slip slip purl decrease.

Bind off loosely. Weave in loose ends.

Finishing

Pin panels together with right sides up and panel 2 in center. Carefully align color block squares when pinning. With yarn A threaded on tapestry needle, sew panels in place using mattress stitch. Rethread

needle as necessary, leaving 4″ (10cm) tails to weave in later. Steam lightly.

With color C threaded on tapestry needle, add decorative whipstitch around squares (see page 24), rethreading needle as necessary. Cut yarn after each horizontal and vertical seam leaving 4″ (10cm) tail to weave in later.

Pin hood to 1 corner of towel with wrong sides together, easing hood edges in order to fit the towel corner. With color C, work 2 rows single crochet around towel edges, working 3 single crochet stitches in each corner stitch to neatly round the corners. Weave in ends to wrong side of work.

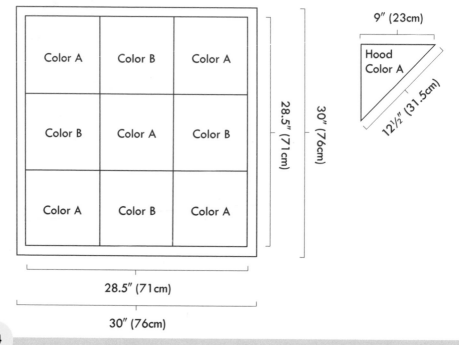

84

Baby Bibs

Baby bibs make a nice gift for a newborn. They knit up quickly and have tons of charm when customized with a sweet little heart or sailboat. Follow the chart to create the design, and this project will be smooth sailing all the way.

Designer: Lucie Sinkler

Size

7×7″ (18×18cm)

What You'll Need

Yarn: 100% cotton light worsted weight or DK weight solid-color yarn, approximately 50 yards (46m) *each bib* (yarn A); 100% cotton light worsted weight or DK weight variegated yarn, approximately 25 yards (23m) *each bib* (yarn B)

We used: Tahki Cotton Classic (100% mercerized cotton; 108 yards [100m] per 1¾oz [50g] skein): #3847, 1 skein (blue bib); #3931, 1 skein (lavender bib); Tahki Tweedy Cotton Classic (100% mercerized cotton; 108 yards [100m] per 1¾oz [50g] skein): #474, 1 skein (boat); #473, 1 skein (heart)

Needles: US size 4 (3.5mm); US size 2 (2.75mm) circular, 24″ (61cm) long

Notions: Stitch holder; tapestry needle

Gauge

26 stitches and 36 rows=4″ (10cm) in stockinette stitch

Notes

• The yarn is worked on small needles in order to produce a closely knit fabric so spills won't soak through easily.

• When changing colors, drop the old color and bring the new color up from under the old color, twisting them together to avoid gaps (see page 21). For the boat pattern you will need 2 balls yarn A and 1 ball yarn B. For the heart you will need 3 balls yarn A and 2 balls yarn B. Because these areas are quite small, you may choose to cut long lengths of yarn instead of winding smaller balls or bobbins.

Make the bib

Using yarn A and size 4 (3.5mm) needles cast on 31 stitches.

Row 1 and all odd-number rows (wrong side): Purl all stitches.

Row 2: Knit 1, make 1, knit 29, make 1, knit 1. (33 stitches)

Row 4: Knit 1, make 1, knit 31, make 1, knit 1. (35 stitches)

Row 6: Knit 1, make 1, knit 33, make 1, knit 1. (37 stitches)

Row 8: Knit 1, make 1, knit 35, make 1, knit 1. (39 stitches)

Row 10: Knit 1, make 1, knit 37, make 1, knit 1. (41 stitches)

Work in stockinette stitch (knit on right side, purl on wrong side) for 7 rows more, ending with row 17.

Next row: Begin working motif (heart or sailboat) following the chart and using the intarsia method (see page 21).

After finishing charted design, work 10 rows in stockinette stitch with yarn A.

Shape neckline

Row 1 (right side): Knit 12, bind off 17, knit to end of row (12 stitches on each side of bind-off). Place first set of 12 stitches on stitch holder.

Rows 2, 4, 6, 8, 10, and 12: Purl.

Row 3: Bind off 2 stitches, knit 10.

Row 5: Bind off 1 stitch, knit to end of row. (9 stitches)

Row 7: Bind off 1 stitch, with 1 stitch already on right needle from bind-off, knit 5 more, knit 2 together. (7 stitches)

Row 9: Bind off 1 stitch, with 1 stitch already on right needle, knit 3 more, knit 2 together. (5 stitches)

Row 11: Bind off 1 stitch, with 1 stitch already on right needle, knit 1 more, knit 2 stitches together. (3 stitches)

Row 13: Slip 2 stitches as if to knit them together, knit 1, pass the 2 slipped stitches over the knitted one. Cut yarn, pull tail through last stitch and fasten off.

Rejoin yarn to 12 stitches on holder and knit other side, reversing shaping.

Edging and ties

With right side facing, pick up 43 stitches along the neckline edge of bib using yarn B and size 2 (2.75mm) circular needles. Knit 3 rows. Bind off all stitches.

With circular needle and using knitted cast-on method and yarn B, cast on 50 stitches. With same needle and yarn and right side facing, pick up 140 stitches evenly along left edge, bottom, and right edge of bib. Cast on another 50 stitches on the end. Knit 3 rows.

Bind off all stitches. Weave in all ends to wrong side of work.

Key
- main color
- contrast color

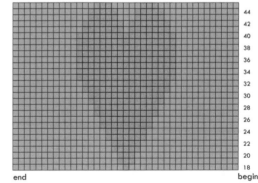

44
42
40
38
36
34
32
30
28
26
24
22
20
18

end   begin

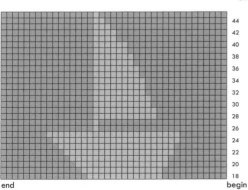

44
42
40
38
36
34
32
30
28
26
24
22
20
18

end   begin

Key
- main color
- contrast color

Baby's Buddy Inchworm Pillow

This cute cushion gently cradles a sleepy child's head. It makes a thoughtful gift that you can create in a day. Knitted up in a soft, washable cottony yarn, it's both snuggly and easy to clean.

Designer: Helen Ralph

Size

Length (after stuffing): about 29″ (73.5cm)

What You'll Need

Yarn: Worsted weight yarn, approximately 127 yards (116m); scrap yarn in assorted colors for eyes, nose, I-cord striping

We used: Rowan All Seasons Cotton (60% cotton, 40% acrylic; 98 yards [90m] per 50g ball): #217 Lime Leaf (yarn A), 2 balls; #219 Duskand (yarn B), 1 ball; Rowan Handknit Cotton (100% cotton; 93 yards [85m] per 50g ball): #319 Mango Fool (yarn C), 1 ball; #215 Rosso (yarn D), 1 ball

Needles: US size 7 (4.5mm); US size 6 (4mm) double-pointed, set of 2

Notions: Stitch holder; long sewing pins; tapestry needle; polyester fiberfill

Gauge

16 stitches and 23 rows=4″ (10cm)

Purl of Wisdom

Choose a cotton/acrylic blend of yarn that combines the pillowy soft texture of cotton with the shape retention of acrylic.

Make the pillow (make 2)

Cast on 16 stitches.

Row 1 (right side): Knit 1, knit into front and back of next stitch, knit across to last 2 stitches, knit into front and back loop, knit 1. (18 stitches)

Row 2 (wrong side): Purl 1, make 1 purl-wise (see page 69), purl across to last stitch, make 1 purlwise, purl 1. (20 stitches)

Rows 3, 5, 7, and 9: Repeat row 1.

Rows 4, 6, 8, and 10: Repeat row 2.

Row 11 (right side): Repeat row 1. (38 stitches)

Row 12: Purl.

Row 13: Knit 1, knit into front and back loop, knit to last 2 stitches, knit into front and back loop, knit 1. (40 stitches)

Rows 14–17: Repeat rows 12 and 13 twice more. (44 stitches)

Row 18: Purl.

Row 19: Knit.

Rows 20–23: Repeat rows 12 and 13 twice more. (48 stitches)

Row 24: Purl.

Row 25: Knit 1, knit into front and back of next stitch, knit 20, knit 2 together, turn work. Continue to work on these 24 stitches only. Place remaining 24 stitches on stitch holder.

Row 26: Bind off 2 stitches, purl to end. (22 stitches on needle)

Row 27: Knit to last 2 stitches, knit 2 together. (21 stitches)

Row 28: Purl.

Row 29: Knit.

Row 30: Bind off 1 stitch, purl to end. (20 stitches)

Row 31: Knit to last 2 stitches, knit 2 together. (19 stitches)

Rows 32–40: Starting with a purl row, work 9 rows in stockinette stitch, ending with a wrong-side row.

Row 41: Knit 2 together, knit to last 2 stitches, knit into front and back loops of next stitch, knit 1. (19 stitches)

Row 42: Purl.

Row 43: Knit to last 2 stitches, knit into front and back loops of next stitch, knit 1. (20 stitches)

Row 44: Purl.

Row 45: Knit 2 together, knit to last stitch, knit into front and back loops of last stitch. (20 stitches)

Row 46: Purl.

Row 47: Knit to last stitch, knit into front and back loops of last stitch. (21 stitches)

Row 48: Purl.

Row 49: Knit 2 together, knit to end. (20 stitches)

Rows 50 and 51: Repeat rows 48 and 49 once. (19 stitches)

Row 52: Purl.

Row 53: Knit 2 together, knit to last 2 stitches, knit 2 together. (17 stitches)

Rows 54–61: Repeat rows 52–53 four times. (9 stitches)

Row 62: Bind off 1 stitch, purl to last 2 stitches, purl 2 together. (7 stitches)

Row 63: Knit 2 together, knit to last 2 stitches, knit 2 together. (5 stitches)

Bind off remaining stitches. Cut yarn.

Pick up 24 stitches from stitch holder, and work the pattern from row 25, reattaching yarn and reversing all shaping. ***Note:*** Beginning the second section with a knit (right-side) row, the shaping that involved binding off stitches on the wrong side (rows 26, 30, 62) in the first section will now change to purl 2 together for each bind-off stitch called for in the pattern as you will not be able to bind off at the end of a purl row without cutting the yarn. For example, row 62 will now begin and end with purl 2 together.

Finishing

Press both pieces using plenty of steam to gently block into shape, smoothing edges to form even curves. Do not stretch the knitting. Pin together with wrong sides facing, matching all edges. With yarn A threaded on tapestry needle, use mattress stitch to sew the pieces together around the edges, leaving an opening at the head or tail for the filling. Stuff the pillow as evenly as possible; do not overstuff. Stitch opening shut, tie yarn tail into knot, and weave in ends to inside of pillow.

Adding features

Note: Stitch the details into the face using photo as your guide. Knot the tails firmly, pulling loose ends deep into the pillow.

Make the stripe: With yarn C, cast 3 stitches onto 1 double-point needle and make a simple I-cord about 1 yard (91.5m) long (see page 22). To ensure cord is long enough, wrap it around the pillow in a spiral from head to tail. Unwrap. Bind off I-cord and cut yarn. Pin one end of cord to the underside of the pillow, about 3″ (7.5cm) from the tail end. Rewrap cord around worm, ending on the underside about 3″ (7.5cm) from head end, and pin it into place. Hide end of cord underneath spiral. Using yarn C threaded onto tapestry needle, stitch cord into place along entire length to secure it to the pillow, adding a backstitch every few stitches. Hide all stitches underneath the cord, with yarn tails knotted firmly and pulled deep into the body of the pillow.

Make the antennae: Cut 6 pieces of yarn A each about 8″ (20.5cm) in length. Thread 3 pieces onto tapestry needle and draw yarn halfway through a stitch where the first antenna will be. Remove needle, leaving yarn pulled halfway through stitches. With about 4″ (10cm) on both sides, braid the yarn. Finish by knotting strands together firmly. Trim yarn tails to desired length. Repeat with the remaining 3 pieces of yarn for the other antenna.

Make the eyes: Thread 24″ (61cm) yarn B onto tapestry needle, pull ends together and tie in overhand knot to create a 12″ (30.5cm) double strand. Pull yarn through a stitch about 1″ (2.5cm) below first antenna, and thread needle between strands at knot. Pull yarn gently to anchor, and push knot behind stitches. Make eye using a satin stitch, going across 3 knit rows. Make 3 or 4 stitches next to each other, creating an oval for the eye. Run needle up through the back of the stitches made, and push the needle deep into the stuffing of the head and across to where you will make the other eye. Repeat instructions to make second eye. After you've run the needle up through the back of the stitches just made, cut yarn at needle. Knot ends, rethread needle with yarn ends, and pull yarn and knot through stitches to hide inside body. Remove needle.

Make the nose: Make a 1½″ pom-pom (see page 29). Thread tapestry needle with yarn tails, draw through 3 stitches at the position desired, and pull the nose into place. Draw the needle through the pillow a few times more to firmly anchor nose to face; knot yarn securely. Hide knot behind nose.

Purl of Wisdom

If you don't want to make a pom-pom, stitch a nose following the steps for making the eyes.

Fancy Stitch Pullover

Don't let the fancy color work fool you—this fun and bright pullover is a cinch to knit and will wow everyone who sees it.

Designer: Beth Walker-O'Brien

Size

1 year: chest 25" (63.5cm), length 12½" (32cm)

2 years: chest 27" (68.5cm), length 13" (33cm)

3 years: chest 29" (74cm), length 13½" (34.5cm)

What You'll Need

Yarn: Chunky weight yarn, about 500 [700, 880] yards (457m [640m, 804m])

We used: Muench Yarns Tessin (43% superwash wool, 35% acrylic, 22% cotton); 110 yards [100m] per 100g skein): #805 Bright Red (color A), 2 skeins; #808 Royal Blue (color B), 2 skeins; #806 Lively Lime Green (color C), 2 skeins; #839 Chiffon Yellow (color D), 2 skeins

Needles: US size 8 (5mm); US size 10 (6mm); US size 8 (5mm) circular, 12" (30.5cm) or 16" (40.5cm) long

Notions: 3 stitch holders; tapestry needle

Gauge

17 stitches and 22 rows=4" (10cm) in Four-Color Fancy Stitch

Note: Instructions are given for smallest size; numbers for larger sizes are in brackets. When only 1 number is given, it applies to all sizes.

Four-Color Fancy Stitch Pattern

Row 1 (wrong side): With color A, purl across.

Row 2: With color B, knit 2, *slip 1 with yarn in back, knit 1; repeat from * until 1 stitch remains, knit 1.

Row 3: With color B, purl 2, *slip 1 with yarn in front, purl 1; repeat from * until 1 stitch remains, purl 1.

Row 4: With color C, knit 1, *slip 1 with yarn in back, knit 1; repeat from * until 1 stitch remains, knit 1.

Row 5: With color C, purl across.

Row 6: With color D, knit 1, *slip 1 with yarn in back, knit 3; repeat from * until 2 stitches remain, slip 1 with yarn in back, knit 1.

Row 7: With color D, purl 1, *slip 1 with yarn in front, purl 3; repeat from * until 2 stitches remain, slip 1 with yarn in front, purl 1.

Row 8: With color B, knit 2, *slip 3 with yarn in back, knit 1; repeat from * until 1 stitch remains, knit 1.

Row 9: With color B, purl 3, *slip 1 with yarn in front, purl 3; repeat from * until end of row.

Row 10: With color A, knit 1, *slip 1 with yarn in back, knit 3; repeat from * until 2 stitches remain, slip 1 with yarn in back, knit 1.

Repeat rows 1–10 for pattern.

Make the sweater

Back

With size 8 (5mm) needles and color B, cast on 55 [59, 63] stitches.

Row 1: Purl.

Row 2: Knit.

Repeat rows 1 and 2 twice more.

With size 10 (6mm) needles and color A, work the Four-Color Fancy Stitch pattern starting with row 1.

Continue in pattern until piece measures 12½″ [13″, 13½″] (32cm [33cm, 34.5cm]) from start of stitch pattern. Place stitches on holder.

Front

Work same as for back until piece measures 11″ (28cm) ending on a wrong-side row.
Next row (right side): Work 23 [25, 26] stitches in pattern, bind off 9 [9, 11] stitches, work in pattern to end of row. (23 [25, 26] stitches each side of neck)

Shape right side of neck opening (as worn)
Rows 1, 3, and 5 (wrong-side rows): Work across in pattern.
Row 2: Bind off 3 stitches, work across remaining stitches in pattern. (20 [22, 23] stitches)
Row 4: Bind off 2 stitches, work across remaining stitches in pattern. (18 [20, 21] stitches)
Row 6: Knit 1, slip slip knit decrease, work across remaining stitches in pattern. (17 [19, 20] stitches)
Row 7: Work across in pattern.

Repeat rows 6 and 7 twice more. (15 [17, 18] stitches)

Work even in pattern until piece measures 12½″ [13″, 13½″] (32cm [33cm, 34.5cm])

in length from beginning of stitch pattern. Place shoulder stitches on holder.

Shape left side of neck opening (as worn)
Row 1 (wrong side): Join new yarn, bind off 3 stitches and work across remaining stitches in pattern. (20 [22, 23] stitches)
Row 2: Work across in pattern.
Row 3: Bind off 2 stitches, work across remaining stitches in pattern. (18 [20, 21] stitches)
Row 4: Work across in pattern until 3 stitches remain, knit 2 together, knit 1. (17 [19, 20] stitches)
Row 5: Work across in pattern.

Repeat rows 4 and 5 twice more (15 [17, 18] stitches)

Work even in pattern until piece measures 12½″ [13″, 13½″] (32cm [33cm, 34.5cm]) from beginning of stitch pattern. Place shoulder stitches on holder.

Sleeves (make 2)

With size 8 (5mm) needles and color B, cast on 27 [27, 31] stitches.
Row 1: Purl.
Row 2: Knit.

Repeat rows 1 and 2 twice more.

Change to size 10 (6mm) needles and work Four-Color Fancy Stitch pattern while at the same time working make 1 increases on each side of sleeve every fourth row 13 [14, 13] times (53 [55, 57] stitches). Continue in pattern until sleeve length measures 9½" [10", 10½"] 24cm [25.5cm, 26.5cm]. Bind off loosely.

Repeat for second sleeve.

Finishing

Seam left shoulder stitches of front to left shoulder stitches of back using 3-needle bind-off technique. Seam right shoulder stitches using the same method.

Work neckband

With size 8 (5mm) circular needle and color B, with right side facing pick up 54 [54, 56] stitches evenly around neck edge. Join into round. Knit 6 rounds, bind off loosely.

Sew sleeves to body using backstitch, and sew side and sleeve seams using mattress stitch. Weave all loose ends into wrong side of sweater.

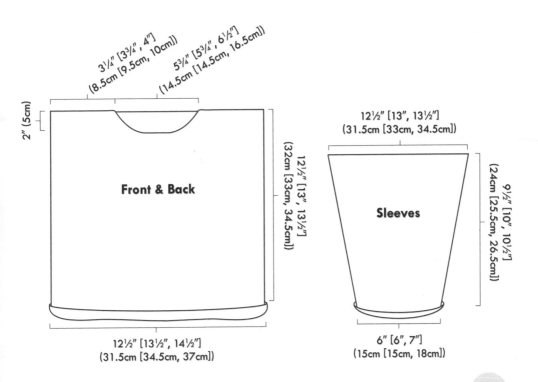

3¼" [3¾", 4"] (8.5cm [9.5cm, 10cm])

5¾" [5¾", 6½"] (14.5cm [14.5cm, 16.5cm])

2" (5cm)

Front & Back

12½" [13", 13½"] (32cm [33cm, 34.5cm])

12½" [13½", 14½"] (31.5cm [34.5cm, 37cm])

12½" [13", 13½"] (31.5cm [33cm, 34.5cm])

Sleeves

9½" [10", 10½"] (24cm [25.5cm, 26.5cm])

6" [6", 7"] (15cm [15cm, 18cm])

Designer Directory

Lesley Edmondson
Wool and Company
23 South Third St.
Geneva, IL 60134
Phone: (630) 232-2305
Fax: (630) 232-2676
www.woolandcompany.com
e-mail: info@woolandcompany.com

Chrissy Gardiner
Gardiner Yarn Works
Portland, OR
Phone: (503) 922-0168
www.gardineryarnworks.com
e-mail: cgardiner@gardineryarnworks.com

Susan Leitzsch
Handknits at Sunrise
11 Sunrise Road
Boonton Township, NJ 07005
e-mail: sueleitzsch@yahoo.com

Kathy Perry
Kathy Perry Designs
e-mail: kperryca@earthlink.net

Helen Ralph
Knit-O-Rama!
Scotland
www.knit-o-rama.com
e-mail: helen@knit-o-rama.com

Lucie Sinkler
CloseKnit, Inc.
622 Grove St.
Evanston, IL 60201
Phone: (847) 328-6760
Fax: (847) 328-0618
e-mail: closeknit@sbcglobal.net

Cathleen Stephen
Knits With a Twist
73 Park Road
Wyomissing Hills, PA 19609
Phone: (484) 529-1753
e-mail: knitswithatwist@aol.com

Beth Walker-O'Brien
Knits Illustrated
Phone: (630) 841-3360
www.knitsillustrated.com
e-mail: beth@knitsillustrated.com